I0199751

We're Just Novices

We're Just Novices

MICHAEL POMEDLI

RESOURCE *Publications* · Eugene, Oregon

WE'RE JUST NOVICES

Copyright © 2024 Michael Pomedli. All rights reserved. Except for brief quotations in critical publications or reviews, no part of this book may be reproduced in any manner without prior written permission from the publisher. Write: Permissions, Wipf and Stock Publishers, 199 W. 8th Ave., Suite 3, Eugene, OR 97401.

Resource Publications
An Imprint of Wipf and Stock Publishers
199 W. 8th Ave., Suite 3
Eugene, OR 97401

www.wipfandstock.com

PAPERBACK ISBN: 979-8-3852-2606-1
HARDCOVER ISBN: 979-8-3852-2607-8
EBOOK ISBN: 979-8-3852-2608-5
VERSION NUMBER 07/03/24

To all the Benedictines
of St Peter's Abbey

Contents

Introduction | ix

Entering the monastery | 1
Snuffing: to laugh or not to laugh? | 2
The porcupine's dilemma | 10
More on intimate relationships | 16
Black Madonna | 21
New names | 22
Reading | 31
Monastic garb: the habit | 36
Work is prayer, prayer is work | 38
The Divine Office | 63
The *Tyrocinium* | 71
Benedictine vows | 85
Benedictine medal | 90
Art and monastic life | 93
Antiquarian nature of the monastery | 96
The liturgical year | 103
Teachings on the mystical body and liturgy | 119
More on the liturgy | 122
Hermit life | 123
Night lights | 126
Less than serious talk | 127
The future | 130
Conclusion | 136

Introduction

A BUSINESS MANAGER, AN artist, a farmer, and a former drug user join a community. No, this is not a setup for a joke. These are real people who choose to live together for a year.

They rise at 4:40 every morning to meditate, remain silent for long periods of time, and obey a superior without hesitation. *We're Just Novices* gives a glimpse into these lives. A master guides them. Their differences unfold during a routine of prayer and work. It is the late 1950s in a prairie monastery and these novices have little contact with the outside world.

Written mainly from the perspective of a single monk, without self-pity and even with a certain merriment, this story traces the simple ideal for those entering a Benedictine community–eat, sleep, and pray. But there are challenges: the rigor of learning to read Latin publicly, the smell of unwashed bodies, earthy humor, dealing with sexual desires, praying without many distractions. In a setting where personal life and private possessions become part of community–a kind of communism–these aspiring individuals pursue their spiritual journeys.

There were good days and there were bad days. This was a good day. It was the beginning of a one-year apprenticeship in the monastery, a year of preparation and scrutiny, both by the monastic community and by these individuals. Those living that whole year together were called novices and that institution was called a novitiate. That year was just before the Catholic church's reform-minded sessions of Vatican Council II (1962–65), an important time for the people of God.

It was a year of conformity, for the emphasis in the church and monastery was on right order, keeping the rules, which were generally in line with the church as a whole and with the mostly post-German origins of this prairie monastic community.

There were trials, hopes and disappointments. It was a time to get their feet wet in the monastic life, to understand themselves and their vocation. This striving took place not only on the personal level, but in a religious community in interaction with others. The closest others were fellow novices; the more extended others were the monastic community.

Although often written in the first-person singular, this account is not entirely, or mostly, about Frater Tobias. This novitiate occurred during a watershed time, for while some reforms were already anticipated, rigors of the past remained. It was a formative time, a time of unquestioning obedience which was mitigated somewhat after that year elapsed and former novices pursued monastic-seminary studies.

Novices were formed according to an exacting pattern; they began like a planted seed; during the novitiate and after, they had to germinate and grow, moving from narrow straits to unrealized dreams, but with the psalmist they were full of sap and still green.

The chaplain at the monastery's boys' high school, chilled would-be novices about a romantic idea of life in the monastery. For him, St. Benedict's Rule was a directive for beginners. Monastic life was like a river flowing along, sometimes faster, sometimes slower, sometimes warmer and sometimes colder. On its banks there were trees to give shade and comfort, but also rocks to hinder.

What gave a touch of realism to any romantic ideas about monastic life was the monastery/college building and its grounds. The four-story red brick building was rather imposing, designed by an architectural firm from Milwaukee, but it formed only one-quarter of a proposed medieval-European quadrangle with a huge twin-spired church. In place of the model was a plain and restrained building, a miniature of the whole, but nevertheless it took the community more than 20 years to erase the mortgage despite the procurator/business manager's efforts at frugality. The chaplain stated that he was reluctant to replace the working Brothers' worn-out gloves and prescribed that monks use only two squares of toilet paper. That sparseness was still evident now but it gave a hint of serenity, even severity, since the grass was unmanicured and flower beds only semi-attended to.

The same large door to both the monastery and the college opened onto a porch and yawning cavities forward and upward. An open door into a closed society?

This high school chaplain noted that this Order provided a balanced program for monks so they became and stayed human. The obedience required could be seen as restrictive but also as liberating, as an end to personal freedom, but also as the beginning of a release. The Rule could be constraining and narrowing but also as an aid to growth.

Benedictines were not known for their heroism, spiritual or otherwise, the chaplain continued, unlike members of other Orders. There were no gold medalists among them. Their spirituality could be envisioned as ordinary and even tedious, their prayer and work, not primarily that of individuals but that of a community. But in this togetherness there was possible growth and depth, a holiness, the sanity of a well-tempered life. The Benedictines were like a team of mountaineers searching for a spiritual summit together, discovering themselves in concert with others.

Entering the monastery

FOUR NOVICES ENTERED A monastic community. All male. A motley crew, nevertheless.

Was it fate or God's grace that brought them together? No, it couldn't have been grace for their intentions were not always pure and noble. Or does grace move within and beyond impurities?

They entered the monastery in the late 1950s when the Soviet Union launched Sputnik, the first artificial earth satellite. The director of novices, Father Martin, was excited to bring them this news. Sputnik was only two feet in diameter, travelled at 18,000 miles an hour, and orbited for three weeks before falling back to earth. Father Martin showed a picture of the satellite, a polished metal sphere with four antennae to broadcast radio signals. Its path covered virtually the entire earth. "The Russians beat the Americans!" Father Martin exclaimed.

The Americans tried to catch up to the Soviets with their Vanguard satellite. Father Martin announced almost with glee that Vanguard exploded shortly after liftoff, a humiliation to this so-called world leader in science and technology. The press pronounced it a Kaputnik, an Oopsnik or Flopnik. A few weeks later, however, the American Explorer succeeded in another liftoff.

Snuffing: to laugh or not to laugh?

AT LEAST ONE OF the monks did some snuffing. He did not chew it or spit while using this smokeless tobacco. There are two ways of snuffing: one is to sniff tobacco up one's nostrils and the other is to use it in plug form and put it somewhere in one's mouth, between the lower lip and teeth, for instance.

Frater Tobias recalled that when he was teaching in high school, one of his older students who sat in the front row, snuffed. Initially, he was not aware of his habit. One time during class, he abruptly went to the waste basket and spit into it. He did it so quickly that Frater Tobias and fellow students hardly noticed. He apologized after class, noting that he had too much phlegm in his mouth and had to excrete some of it. He would try not to do it again. Frater Tobias did not voice any objection to his snuffing.

But here were the novices in the monastery faced with a few regular snuffers. In days past, one of the monks said that snuffing was very common and acceptable. During celebrations of high Mass, for instance, monk presiders regularly and ritually took time out to snuff, mostly just before the dismissal.

Although the novices were aware that the Prior of the monastery snuffed, they became more acutely aware of this during one incident. After one of the novices had served the Abbot's Mass, the second Mass of the day for the novices, they were meditating in their pews when Father Prior entered his prayer stall after his private Mass, sat down, and in ritual fashion, took out his snuff box, tapped on the lid, opened it, removed a pinch of snuff, inserted some into each nostril, breathed it in, took out his red, polka-dotted bandana handkerchief and loudly snorted the excess snuff into it. Droppings fell at his choir place.

The novices were aware of this procedure, but this time something different happened. As the Prior took the snuff box out of his habit pocket and removed the lid, that lid escaped his grasp; he grabbed for this cover but only succeeded in propelling it down the aisle that separated the two choirs. It clinked down the aisle toward the altar, hit the altar step and clanged as it spun around and settled on the floor. Novices were awakened from their prayer reverie and responded to the incident with fitful and uncontainable laughs that continued for some time.

Just then Father Abbot returned from his private Mass and wondered what the melee was about. Novices noticed his anxious and distressed face. They thought nothing further of this chapel incident and slowly returned to their normal serious state, but continued to feel the effect of this humorous moment. That, however, was not the end. After breakfast, Father Abbot called the four to his office and lectured them on the seriousness of what they had done: they had laughed at the dear Prior and should never do that again. The Prior was engaging in a time-honored custom and the novices trivialized it. Father Abbot was obviously angry; he did not repress it but managed it quite well. As a penance for their misdeed, each novice was commanded to recite privately the seven *Penitential Psalms*. All things considered, the reprimand was not so bad, the penance quite lenient, and the fun relished.

But the event provoked the interest in snuffing for Frater Tobias. He had a hard time finding information on it since novices had limited access to print material. He found out that historically, there were many advocates of snuffing who noted the positive spiritual and health benefits of nicotine, for it was reputed to help focus the mind and calm the nerves. Historically, the Roman church swayed back and forth in its judgment about the use of snuff. Converts in the New World had to be dissuaded from continuing their habits of snuffing, especially during church ceremonies. In the seventeenth century, Pope Urban VIII wrote a Bull (a public letter) against the use of tobacco by mouth or nose; he was concerned about imbibing whole portions, whether pieces, shredded, or powder, and threatened those who used it with excommunication. For him, such snuffing defiled the user and the sacred precincts. There was an account of a priest in Naples who snuffed after communion and fell into a fit of sneezing, vomited on the altar, and horrified the congregation.

This Bull was later revoked since popes were now among the snuffers. In recent history there were notable snuffers and providers: St. Padre Pio, a

3

habitual user, and St. Bernadette Soubirous who used snuff for her asthma; in Central and South America, the Jesuits owned tobacco plantations and therefore condoned the use of snuff. Pope Pius IX, Pio Nono, gave telltale evidence of clerical snuffing; his white habit, used since Dominican days, was often soiled with tobacco juice!

Frater Tobias also uncovered a debate whether snuffing would break one's fast from food and drink. The debate ended on an indulgent note that even if some juice entered the stomach, the fast would not be broken, provided the greater amount of juice was spit out.

Apart from the incident with Father Prior, the four novices were a rather humorless bunch and the rest of the monastery with them. From casual associations with older monks, however, novices learned that the absence of jocularity was not the case in earlier days. Playing practical jokes, and a lightsome feeling, especially during the hunt for deer, and often accompanied by alcohol, were commonplace then.

Jesus and God are often portrayed as stern and humorless. Frater Tobias wondered whether that was the case, so he checked a biblical concordance (an index of words) for instances of joking and humor and found quite a few positive examples: in the Latin psalms that monks pray daily, for instance, Psalm 2, "the One whose throne is in heaven sits laughing" at warring nations; Psalm 32, "Rejoice in Yahweh, exult, you virtuous, shout for joy, all upright hearts;" Psalm 37, God laughs at the wicked person. So, God has a sense of humor and this novice thought we should take a great deal of delight in that.

In the *Book of Proverbs,* he found that wisdom provided guidance for her people but they ignored her and she then laughed at their consequent distress; also, "a glad heart is excellent medicine, a spirit depressed wastes the bones away."

Frater Tobias liked the *Hebrew Testament* depiction of joking concerning Abraham and Sarah. Old man Abraham laughed at God's promise that he would father a child. God found it funny, for he fulfilled his promise to provide prolific progeny—as many as the sands of the sea—to this elderly couple. The product of this pregnancy was called Isaac, which means laughter. So, God not only tolerated the couple's laughter but joined in it, herself/himself. Like God, and Abraham and Sarah, this novice concluded that we have to laugh more at our bodies, our functions with their limitations and capabilities, learn to be humble, for humor is from *humus,* earth. In conclusion, we should not take ourselves too seriously.

In the *New Testament,* during the Sermon the Mount, Jesus indicates that happiness, which includes laughter, is a foretaste of the blessings of the kingdom of God. Even those who do not have many possessions are enjoined to be happy, as well as those who mourn, seek justice, are peacemakers and those who are persecuted. We might not see all the positive effects of the kingdom on earth, but should strive for them for we are hopeful that they will be realized to some measure in the future.

God must have had fun in creating such a vast universe, and the Father and Spirit must have rejoiced at the begetting and birth of Jesus. Frater Tobias still remembered the outburst novices showed when the Prior's snuff top wangled its way up the aisle, but then he read that in his Rule, Benedict seemed to be against such goofing off. Well, goofing off does seem a bit irrational; but was he against laughing? He wrote: "The eleventh step of humility is that a monk speaks gently and without laughter, seriously and with becoming modesty, briefly and reasonably, but without raising his voice, as it is written: 'A wise man is known by his few words.'" And in the tenth step of humility, he quotes *Ben Sirach:* "Only a fool raises his voice in laughter."

Was Benedict against all forms of laughter, or when he castigates laughter, did he mean the process of laughing at someone, rather than with someone, that is, hurtful laughter? Surely one can use proper humor to defuse anger. But anger should also be permitted and be observable for it is a legitimate monastic emotion, even at funerals. Tears at a monastic funeral? Oh, no, no tears. Why should there be? In monastic life, it seems there is room only for order and reason.

Monks should have everything in place, even their deaths. Here, Father Martin elicited a saying, *subitanea mors, clericorum sors,* a sudden death is the lot of a cleric. "I guess these words also apply to the Brothers, even though they are not priests," he commented. "The monastic cemetery is a clear indication of the logic of order and preparedness: tombstones are arranged in straight lines and clearly marked, the lawn well kept, and trimmed evergreens and hedges encircle these final, peaceful resting places. It is a serene place for repose and not for wild emotions. In keeping with this serenity, there are no flowers during monastic funerals, only a simple wooden casket, one made, early on, in the carpenter shop, even one made by and for the carpenter himself."

So, monks never cried during a burial. No, not even a tear for beloved Father Bernard, just a somber and morose attitude at the funeral of this pastor-monk who died during this novitiate. There was no silence during the meal following the funeral, however, and wine, laughter and verbal sharing lightened hearts and made everyone feel much better.

There was a grand obituary of Father Bernard in the *Messenger*. In its pages, priests and nuns got all the accolades for they seemed to do no wrong. But there was also one of a parish housekeeper, Anna, an atypical one. It noted that she had a giddy disposition but could not tell a good joke to save her life. However, that didn't matter since her many attempts at joke-telling were infinitely funnier than the jokes she was trying to tell. She was a scatter brain and chaotic, writing everything down and then losing track of her notes. Once having spent a month wearing a strange pair of glasses, she later discovered she had salvaged them from the parish parking lot.

There was a death notice about a prominent lay person who was educated by the Benedictines. This detailed notice was seemingly written by a Benedictine, maybe with tongue in cheek: "His life's work was to reject the clergy, one of his many irresistible urges to be outrageous. Even in high school, he exhibited an increasing traumatic adolescence as he pulled a prank or two on the men in black; one time he placed a small charge of nitrogen triiodide close to the prefect's presiding desk. He must have taken it from the chemistry lab; since it was an extremely sensitive contact explosive, it banged with a loud, sharp snap when the prefect touched it, releasing a purple cloud of iodine vapor. Wow! This nixnuts became a teacher but exhibited cognitive defects, administrative missteps and had a small-town mentality. He loved gardening but while doing so was run down by a charging bull moose. He showed an interest in the mad trapper because both shared the same background. He died of pulmonary self-abuse, the oldest in his family, the first to ripen and the first to rot."

Frater Tobias remembered a mandated silence during one of his philosophy classes. The professor wanted students to savor some unique experiences and so asked them to be silent for three minutes and take note of this episode. As the period began, one of the students, late, of course, barged into the classroom, looked around apprehensively as the professor bade her sit down for all were observing a period of silence. Another student started munching on an apple but stopped abruptly for his biting was quite loud.

Many students felt awkward at such an unusual interval. After the three minutes had elapsed, they shared their experiences. For some it was very novel, for they spoke of listening to their heartbeat, to ambient noises outside, to feeling a bonding in this condition. A few years later when Frater

Tobias met his professor again, he remarked that this silent period was the most memorable moment in the entire class! The professor received this comment with a smile.

Again, was St. Benedict against all forms of laughter, for it can lighten the heart and make everyone feel much better.

According to the Rule, the proud person raises his voice to drown out others. Such a loud-mouth tries to control others and impose himself in every situation, surely not an indication of humility. Joking around and laughing loudly can be a way of controlling the disposition of others.

The gentleness that Benedict wrote about shows a marked preference for quietness, taking his cue from the *Gospel of Matthew* where Jesus says that we should learn from him for he is "gentle and humble of heart." Then we shall find rest for our souls.

Based on his personal experience in seeking God and his spiritual guidance of others, Benedict put a lot of emphasis on silence, devoting all of chapter six to it. His emphasis is not on total silence for then we would have to learn sign language and use it constantly. He suggested a disposition or habit of silence during which there might be some noise and speaking, and obviously monks should avoid misusing the tongue. He also advised instilling the mood of following God in peace and quiet and building a disposition toward better relationships in the community.

Such dispositions and actions would enable monks not to disturb others but preeminently help them listen to the voice of God, to slow down, get still and find God and grace.

"Other orders put more emphasis on silence than do the Benedictines," Father Martin stated, "for we are into moderation. But we still covet silence for then we can journey into the spiritual realm, lead a life of meditation, get a genuine divine connection, and refuel our spirituality."

But Frater Tobias still thought the novices were right in laughing at the Prior's foibles.

In the Gospels Jesus shows his sense of humor in his penchant for exaggeration. Again, this is especially true in his Sermon on the Mount where he examines a standard for treating others and being judged ourselves. He makes fun of the person who worries about the speck in his brother's eye but overlooks the log in his own. Yes, see the speck of sand or dust in the other's eye but also the telephone pole in your own. Yes, it is so easy to pick at another's faults and not acknowledge our own.

Like the Prior's snuff box caper, novices found another amusing incident, this time involving Father Abbot. During recreation time and before
the 7:30 evening prayers, some of the monks, including the Abbot, went to
the bathroom. After he completed this function, the Abbot always preceded
everyone up the stairs to the chapel. Somehow in the bathroom, the Abbot's
habit got hitched in his underwear and he led the way with this rear-end
flourish. The Abbot was somewhat deaf and he did not hear the snickers
from his fellow monks about his pent-up drawers as they processed slowly
to solemn prayers. Consequently, there were no *Penitential Psalms* mandated at this event!

Frater Tobias treasured Jesus' delight in exaggeration. He poked fun
at the legalistic Pharisees who strained out a gnat but swallowed a camel.
Imagine, such an obsessive-compulsive person straining out a small insect
from his soup bowl but swallowing a huge hump back camel. Well, no, that
is an exaggeration. But the Pharisees certainly focused on externals and
missed the large picture, emphasized trivialities but not weightier matters.
They wanted to do everything by the book but were not available to help the
needy. Hyperbole was Jesus' way of getting his point across.

So, it is "easier for a camel to go through the eye of a needle than
for a rich man to enter the kingdom of heaven." Actually, according to a
scripture commentator, the Aramaic word for camel can also mean a large
rope. So, according to this rendition, it is easier to pull a large rope through
the eye of a needle than. . .

This type of dispossession for the rich or relativizing of possessions
was brought home to the novices before they entered the novitiate. They
were to bring a minimum of items. So, prized possessions were left behind,
especially, for Frater Tobias, that compact tube radio that his Mom and Dad
gave him for his grade twelve graduation, all of the records of his achievements in high school, particularly his athletic pennants.

Novices realized that this community was like an ideal communism
where there was a relative equality of persons, where individual possessions
became common property, where each monk was given what was needed
and challenged to give according to his ability.

Maybe Jesus' humor was possible because he had a certain naivete.
There is reason to doubt whether Jesus was character savvy. He could have
chosen someone with greater intelligence and stability than Simon as his
leader and confidante; he strangely renamed him Peter which means rock
and then vowed to build his church on that rock. Peter sank like a rock

when he tried to walk on water; he was so slow to grasp Jesus' basic teachings, asked what he could receive by following him; he was a character full of flaws, more like sand, sandy, rather than rocky and solid.

He boasted that he would stay with Jesus even when others fled but fell asleep twice when Jesus asked him to stay awake and pray with him; he denied knowing him three times. However, there might have been more wisdom than naivete in Jesus for he had a deeper insight into Peter than the rest of the disciples; he was a pillar of the early church.

The resurrection is perhaps the greatest joke. The empty tomb. Not what you would expect. The Church Fathers thought it was a joke on Satan for it was a great reversal–that death is not the end. Jesus is risen, the best reason to laugh, to be joyful, to drink and feast.

The porcupine's dilemma

THE NOVICE MASTER GINGERLY broached the topic of intimacy and distance in relationships. At first, he confessed that negative and a-hands-off approach were not adequate. He wondered how novices could navigate the desire both for closeness and that of respectful distance without isolating and unduly harming themselves. In fact, he had read about this problem.

From his studies in philosophy, he brought up the challenge posed by Arthur Schopenhauer as the hedgehog's or porcupine's dilemma. While porcupines huddle together in winter to prevent freezing to death, their huddling eventually leads to harm as they poke each other with their sharp quills. So, they stay apart, but carefully come together again, a detached waltz and then together.

Schopenhauer wondered what the optimal distance and closeness is. "So, we monks wonder how close we should be to one another and how separated. Those of us who are cozy by ourselves tend to isolate a lot and therefore do not get pricked and do not prick others, but we also need the warmth of others. The dilemma is how to achieve a balance as monks and as professionals so that we remain close enough to fulfill social needs and give support and yet set boundaries in this sharing.

"Different people will behave differently; some feel more comfortable with a greater distance and others in a closer relationship. Social gatherings show this jockeying for closeness and distance even in conversations. Not abiding by this rule is a sure recipe for disaster. Married couples have this problem acutely, often leading to separation and divorce.

"When it is warm outside, we might manage this distance better than when we stay inside a lot of the time. Remaining inside for long periods of time and being reserved, however, might affect our mental health.

Somehow in the monastery all of us want to remain connected as friends, but we also want to support the need for distance, maintaining a sense of well-being while minimizing physical closeness.

"The preacher in the *Book of Ecclesiastes* gives this advice: 'Better two than one by himself, since thus their work is really profitable. If one should fall, the other helps him up; but woe to the man by himself with no one to help him up when he falls down. Again, they keep warm who sleep two together, but how can a man keep warm alone? Where one alone would be overcome, two will put up resistance; and a threefold cord is not quickly broken.'

"To me it's unclear how we remain in this dynamic state in a way that maximizes the benefit of familiarity and the need for space. I can't really solve the porcupine dilemma mathematically for it depends on the dynamic interplay of balancing our risk tolerance as individuals with concern for others and for our community."

In the end, it became obvious that Father Martin chose a very cautious approach to this dilemma. Although the four novices were quite a friendly bunch, or maybe because they were so friendly, Father Martin spoke vigorously and negatively about particular friendships.

"In the recitation of the Divine Office and in spiritual reading, you are reforming the interior man and thereby will arrive at a high degree of religious perfection. But the exterior man also requires attention. In this striving, I take a negative tack using the *Tyrocinium*, a guide for monks: We should avoid undue familiarity with others, detesting all forms of private friendship which spring from the flesh and which seek the pleasure of the flesh alone. We should avoid all forms of hedonism such as music, fashion, and amorality."

Novices wondered whether Father Martin was really serious about this for they noticed that some priests delighted in music and they walked with one another after supper and most of them rather enjoyed it. They also partnered with the same individuals every evening. But novices were advised not to follow their examples of closeness and exclusivity but to have the same attitude and external relationship with each person, that is, be polite, kind, humble, respectful but also somewhat distant.

Father Martin said he did not want to be too detailed on this topic but he did mention that there are tell-tale signs of the depravity of particular relationships, following the *Tyrocinium:* 1. those who cherish this friendship often meet at hidden places and at inappropriate and even forbidden times; they sneak around and do not want to be seen together; 2. they often meet to criticize their confreres and/or their superiors and grumble about how they are ill-treated; 3. they are tattlers, gossiping about others, and thereby destroy peace and excite discord; they are the devil's tools; 4. they form cliques and shun the company of others. 5. they waste valuable time. So, these confabs often breed violations of fraternal charity and peace in the community.

Of course, mutual love is necessary for these brothers because of the common bond through baptism and the ties through religious profession. There are many ways that this care is shown: a cheerful readiness to engage in courteous conversation, for those who remain morose and shun the company of confreres, who are unkind, and are bitter and snappish in speech render themselves unfit for community life. True love should be supernatural, however, that is, directed to God, and not solely to one individual.

Father Martin said that there were some moral theologians who thought that one should ward off any thoughts of close relations with a fellow male. If one engaged in homosexual relations, some theologians concluded, God would get mad at you and you might grow hair on your palms or you might become paralyzed.

During work time, Frater Leo was transparent about his feelings and past actions, although at the same time he admitted to feeling embarrassed about it. "It's like knowing that there are a lot of people in the same boat as you, but you might not admit to being the same as them."

At night, Frater Leo said he had almost uncontrollable urges to engage in genital relationships with males. He told this to his confessor who demanded a general confession of his whole life. He acceded to this, prepared for it and noted the time in his early teens when these urges became more pronounced. He also noted his sudden and terrifying infatuation with a fellow novice sleeping next to him in his private bed. Up to this time, he had not considered the possibility of being a homosexual, but now he thought he might be one and was terrified about it.

His confessor listened attentively, told him to resist such thoughts and actions, for temptations alone are not sinful, and asked him to pray the *Penitential Psalms*. In Frater Leo's judgment, however, this confessor did not understand the situation, at least not the way that he experienced it, and did not give very helpful advice but instead accentuated the problem.

The novice master was not finished with the topic of sexuality. On the day-to-day and practical level, he encouraged the exercise of walking, but with alternate novices instead of the same one and thereby not developing special, close or intimate relationships. During these walks or joggings, Frater Tobias noticed that fellow novices jostled with one another, played with and slapped one another. So, there was some physical stuff going on nevertheless.

Also, during Mass there was a time for the kiss of peace. It was not a kiss in the physical sense, on the lips or cheek, but an embrace, a hug. For many monks this kiss seemed to be a mere formality in the ritual, but for others it seemed to be a sign of intimacy, judging from its duration and closeness. In fact, Frater Tobias thought that from the nature of this kiss of peace, some of the older monks showed an obvious fondness for one another.

"A close embrace during the kiss of peace during Mass," Father Martin said, "is not the intention of the ritual of peace. Rather, it is a sign of chaste brotherly love." But what about a slap on the shoulders during walks? For Frater Leo, the monks did not face the reality that some of them might be homosexuals and becoming a monk might be one of the reasons they entered a monastery of males; these individuals might have same sexual tendencies and consciously or unconsciously enter this exclusive cloister. Many/most were straight heterosexuals, he judged, however, for when they left the monastery and their vows, they wed a female.

During recreation time, Frater Leo continued with this topic. "I have never seen Father Abbot hugging anyone, but two of us were walking past his office/room in the monastery and he happened to come out, saw us, and grabbed our hands and arms in an affectionate gesture. It was a very human action and reaction but was somewhat at variance with what Father Martin had instructed us to do or not to do."

Seemingly without meaning to do so, Father Martin had spent a lot of time on these topics. The temperature was hot outside and also inside and Father Martin rather uncustomarily sat on top of the front of the table from which he was talking. Novices noticed that he was obviously trying to relieve himself of some of the heat for he revealed that he was pantless under his habit. He had not recommended this practice to the novices!

From the fidgeting with his hands and legs, we gathered that Father Martin was a little uneasy in bringing up the necessary topic of sexuality in general, and homosexuality in particular. Perhaps he was doing the talk out of obedience to his superior. His talk became even more serious when it centered on the topic of masturbation. His general hipdediddy tone of voice became softer and even elusive as he began to use the term, unnatural actions, and addressed this experience.

He called masturbation a gravely disordered action, an act against the natural law. Such pleasurable actions should occur only within the bounds of marriage and be oriented toward begetting children, for these pleasures then offset the burdens of child rearing. Unlike marital sexual intercourse, masturbation was not a rational function. This inappropriate desire and action showed a lack of self-control and could have such harmful consequences as, again, growing hair on the palms of one's hands, mental and physical disability, insanity and even death. Because the possible results were so alarming, steps were taken in the nineteenth century to stem masturbation: such young men were sent to mental asylums to receive treatments; physical restraints and sometimes surgery were used to prevent this physical abuse.

Frater Leo dared to ask why masturbation was wrong since he did not understand Father Martin's reasoning. To this novice, it seemed such a common, strong and natural urge and event. Father Martin in turn brought up a passage from the *Book of Genesis,* the so-called sin of Onan. In some detail he described that Onan was bound to follow Jewish tradition when his brother died. According to that tradition, after his brother Er's death, Onan had to engage in sexual intercourse with the widow, Tamar, and beget offspring. Since the progeny from this act would not be regarded as his own, he withdrew after intercourse but before ejaculation and "spilled his semen on the ground."

God apparently was displeased with this action and killed Onan because, presumably, he did not follow Jewish tradition and beget a child. Frater Jerome was not convinced that Onan's sin was really masturbation but an argument for not keeping but violating the Jewish tradition. Father Martin, however, still wanted to say that masturbation was wrong. Sex was created by God for the purpose of procreation and not for the alleviation of concupiscence.

Again, there was some dissension. Frater Leo did not understand the word concupiscence. For him, despite the language, fun was fun. For Father Martin, however, the fun could be involved only if it was part of the intimacy between husband and wife. "In contrast, masturbation is a denial of the design God has for a couple's relationship," Father Martin stated. "While the

Bible does not condemn masturbation as such, it describes sexual fantasies that are not pure but very sinful. The Bible teaches that we are both mind and body and both should be pure. Jesus taught, 'You have heard that it was said, You shall not commit adultery; but I say to you that everyone who looks on a woman to lust for her has committed adultery with her already in his heart.' So, lustful thoughts that do not involve one's spouse are sinful. One should not be mastered by the flesh, not give in to its desires, for such mastery can have great spiritual benefits."

Father Martin recited passages from St. Paul's letters about immorality, although the letters did not mention masturbation specifically. "Flee immorality. Every other sin that a man commits is outside the body, but the immoral man sins against his own body." St. Paul writes about illicit sexual intercourse such as fornication, homosexuality, lesbianism and bestiality "But do not let immorality or any impurity or greed even be named among you, as is proper among saints."

Thus, this topic was closed, and there was a sharing of sorts, for novices were generally not allowed or encouraged to make any comments as Father Martin was speaking nor after his remarks. On the topic of sexuality, Frater Tobias recalled an article he had read. A couple visited a neighbor's home and noticed a charming sculpture in their garden. They called it Who-Who because it looked like an owl. A convent of nuns had commissioned ceramic artist Thomas Kakinuma to fashion a work for them. He presented his creation, Two Nuns in a Storm, in which the eyes of the owl are two nuns. These daughters of Christ, however, refused to accept this sculpture because the nuns depicted were engaged in too intimate an embrace, although it was a fine piece of art and the artist might have had the noblest of intentions. Hence, after its rejection, it found its way into this garden and a measure of appreciation.

More on intimate relationships

ONGOING HOEING JOBS GAVE ample time to discuss whatever topic the novices wanted. Frater Leo disclosed that he had an intimate relationship with a female prior to joining fellow novices in the novitiate. He did not think that the monks at the abbey had much knowledge about this part of his previous life.

"It was a great relationship while it lasted," Frater Leo told fellow confrere, Frater Callistus. "In many ways I miss it; I still have unfinished desires. We were kind of lovers for we were close and face to face, unlike friends who relate to one another side to side. At first, we did a lot of cuddling, massaging one another, stroking in casual physical contact, skin to skin, all in a kind of non-sexual way. I guess you call it petting. We had a mutual understanding of our personal boundaries and respected them. We were close, affectionate and happy. We felt great, physically and mentally, in holding one another.

"Our intimacy progressed, if I can use this language, to more physical and sexual forms but not to intercourse. During our close association with one another, I noticed my significant other approaching me and seemingly wanting to indulge in intercourse. I remember reading about how hormones during a certain part of the month moved a female to ravenously desire sex, a heightened libido. I had to waive her off for I did not want to conceive. Instead, at other times we had oral sex. Our relationship diminished in intensity when she was granted a scholarship and left the area. Then we merely corresponded occasionally. While I am at it, I must tell you that for a while we snorted a ton of cocaine."

"My mother told me that in relationships one should keep three t's: touch, lots of talk, and lots of time. Talk and time, I can understand, but touch is more dicey. What is the right amount of touching?" Frater Tobias questioned.

"Really hot stuff," Frater Jerome directed his remark at Frater Leo. "Did the two of you ever consider wearing chastity belts?"

"Some people care for women and girls but do not carry fantasies of them throughout life," Frater Tobias interjected about Frater Leo's experiences. "I wonder whether you still have such images in your mind and can deprive yourself of them, now that you are in the monastery?"

"I don't know whether that is possible," Frater Leo responded. "Those experiences were dynamite."

"Wow, thanks for sharing your intimacies with me," Frater Callistus responded. "I never experienced anything remotely close as that; my mother was physically close to me and I really liked that. I wonder what kind of relationships might be permitted in this monastery. All of us are men of varying ages and urges, and Father Martin has already given us talks about guarding our eyes and against temptations of the flesh."

Father Martin's talks centered on the temptations that women might provide and the challenges that the Church Fathers and hermits wrote about. He noted that canon law forbids under pain of excommunication the entrance of women or girls into the sacred precincts of the monastery. Novices asked whether that punishment would apply to a female baby if she entered the cloister and he said yes. Novices were brave or foolhardy and asked whether they would sin if they embraced a woman. He fudged a lot, but ended up saying that it depended on our intention and who the female was.

"It is a mark of great holiness to embrace a woman and not give in to one's desires," he concluded.

Novices also observed that one female in particular was a focus for a lot of devotions, that is, the Blessed Virgin Mary. The monastery had a statue of her, so in many ways, she was living in their midst, although depictions of her generally did not emphasize feminine qualities. Father Martin pointed out that she was the epitome of women for monks, for she was pure, open, and obedient to the Holy Spirit. "But don't look at the virgin with dirty minds," he concluded.

"I noticed that there is a lot of emphasis on sin when it came to women and a lot of emphasis on law and morality," Frater Callistus observed. "And then I began to read the *Song of Songs* from the *Old Testament*; love there is very beautiful. How do we bring together the law and that love? Also, from the Gospels, Jesus has a lot of dealings with women and there is a lot of touching going on there.

"Before I came to the monastery, I heard that the Abbot who also takes care of the parishes at confirmation time forbade the holding of dances in his area. In fact, he wrote a special letter in which he likened the intimacy of dancing to a preparation for or simulation of intercourse. I don't think his letter had much effect because dances are still being held. In fact, I heard that one of the monks in a parish does some dancing and the parishioners don't seem to mind it; in fact, they appreciate his being so close to his people. But I also heard that Germans, like many other groups, do not express physical affection to one another, at least not publicly. In fact, I heard that some married couples have sex with their clothes on."

"I read that in some orphanages neighboring mothers visit the orphans," Frater Leo chimed in. "They believe that unless there is some snuggling, the children's lives will be stunted. These mothers point to instances where this stunting happens because of the deprivation of touch."

"Our parish priest told a story of a monk who had kept the law against sexuality very well," Frater Jerome noted, "but as he was dying, he hugged his nurse and said he felt he had really longed for this type of physical touch very much. Being held was such a wonderful new experience. It helped him die a peaceful death."

"I think that men especially are in a pickle regarding touching," Frater Leo came in again. "Obviously they should not be overly sensual in their contacts with males and females, but the pickle is that they might have a hard time being close to females. On the other hand, if they are close to male partners they might be shunned as being homosexuals."

"On the topic of sex," Frater Callistus said, "I remember reading Roch Carrier's collection, *Prayers of a Very Wise Child*; in it is a chapter called Titties Prayer. A seven-year-old boy prays for guidance in matters of the flesh and its weaknesses. Since there is no conversation in his life about such matters, he concludes that it must be a sin to speak about titties or to see them."

"On another topic, I like Roch Carrier's famous Canadian story, The Hockey Sweater," Frater Tobias confessed. It concerns a child's intimacy. A French-Canadian boy is so obsessed with hockey player, Maurice Rocket Richard, that he combs his hair to look like him. After he wears the Rocket's Number 9 red, white and blue Canadien sweater for many years, it becomes too small and threadbare. His mother orders a new one from Eaton's catalogue but receives a hated blue and white Maple Leaf's one instead. He then prays to God to send him right away a hundred million moths to eat up that terrible sweater. In the end, he wears the dreaded enemy sweater but his teammates ostracize him for doing so."

Various memories of affection continued to make a comeback among the novices. "There were some poems that I really liked from grade school," Frater Tobias recounted. "One of them portrayed images like my farm community and the French Canadians that I met once in a while. I remember reading the poem, Little Battise by William Henry Drummond. I had a great fascination for it, especially its broken English: 'You bad leetle boy, not moche you care, How busy you're kipin' your poor gran'pere.'

"Little Bateese was much like me: adventurous, mischievous and carefree. Although I didn't dare carry on with my grandparents as he did, I associated with his sentiments of love for the country and his experiences of hardship. My grandparents came from Hungary and hoped for the greater opportunities that the prairies would provide. They were unassuming like Little Bateese and enjoyed the land and all it contained. Like him, they did not feel at home even in small villages, let alone in a big city. The world I experienced, however, was not as idyllic as Bateese portrayed and a lot dirtier."

CELIBACY

For priests and also for monks, celibacy is supposed to be an advantage; embracing it should be freeing in order to work for God's kingdom. But maybe sexual/genital abstinence can result in a focus on sexuality more than its actual consummation. Frater Tobias was reading about this and some of it was rather funny. A twelfth-century monk, St. Hugh of Lincoln, records the reply he made to a woman who had sought his advice over the impotence of her husband; he advised that this impotent male should be made a monk and then his sexual power would be immediately restored to him!

Monks are caught in a dilemma. They need a woman, and many women, their mother first of all, to bring them into existence and sustain them; also, throughout their monkly existence they will need the services of women. But their immediate lives do not center on women. So, there is a need and also not a need.

While the life of a novice did not entail much contact with women, there were the religious Sisters in the kitchen. Surely, they would not become a preoccupation. But a distraction? There was always the possibility of obsessional thoughts at work or at prayer. Father Martin brought up the example of the monk who put up his cowl, his hood, when he went for a dental appointment so that he would not see women. The fact that Father Martin brought up the issue showed that sexuality/genitality was a fundamental reality. Presumably before the monk joined the monastery he had to deal with this reality. And during his monkly existence he continuously had to cope with it.

One monk related his unconscious sexual language when he was in a high school play. On stage he was to announce the title of Charles Dickens' novel, *A Tale of Two Cities*. Nervous and prone to strange twists, his announcement came out as A Sail of Two Titties!

According to Father Martin celibacy entails the avoidance of deliberate sexual thoughts, feelings, and behavior which are sinful. One must cultivate chastity, an honorable and pure way of living according to one's state in life. In celibacy one gives oneself to God alone with an undivided heart, for the sake of the kingdom. Such "brides of Christ" follow Jesus and St. Paul in leading this superior type of life. He quoted St. Paul: "I should like everyone to be like me [celibate], but everybody has his own particular gifts from God, one with a gift for one thing and another with a gift for the opposite."

Of course, in the history of the church and even today there are celibates, some in name only. But celibacy for priests is not a doctrine, for exceptions can be made, and it can, in principle, be changed at any time by the Pope. Celibacy for monks, however, is mandatory.

Father Martin confessed that he had attractions to the opposite sex and noted that he envied those who were seemingly not attracted to women. These asexual beings, if there really are such, have smooth sailing in the monastery. And then there were males who were attracted to fellow males, a topic he had already considered.

Black Madonna

IN THE CHAPEL WAS a free-standing, upright wooden statue of a black Madonna and infant Jesus. While Father Abbot was visiting the abbey of Einsiedeln in Switzerland, he procured this four-foot statue for his monastery. With braided hair, in a red robe, golden neck band, belt and lower garment detail, she is a replica of a Byzantine figure.

There was speculation about the Madonna dark complexion: she might be dark because she is like the historical Mary, or the statue turned dark due to its aging or because of soot deposits from candle smoke, oil lamps and incense; or she is dark-skinned because of her similarity to pre-Christian deities being re-envisioned as Madonna and child.

Einsiedeln is the one of the oldest and most important places of pilgrimage in Switzerland. With its origin dating to the eleventh century, it was an important stop-over for the pilgrims on their way to Santiago de Compostela. There are stories about the weak, the sick, the disenfranchised, the disempowered, women, strangers, outsiders and foreigners who sought refuge under the Virgin's mantle. Many believed that only the Black Madonna could show the right way for murderers and other criminals. Until the eighteenth century, convicted criminals of Switzerland were able to atone for their guilt and go free if they made a pilgrimage to this holy statue.

"I find that while the statue's origins are shrouded in mystery," Frater Jerome concluded, "the Black Madonna gazes at me with humility, seeming not to have a prominent role, yet she is central to Christianity. I might have to have recourse to her when I become desperate in this monastery!"

"She reminds me of my caring mother," Frater Tobias added. "I am nineteen and miss her a lot."

New names

ONE OF THE FIRST projects that the novice master gave to the four novices was to investigate the meaning of their new names and the saints that were connected to them. Presumably these names, and knowledge about them, would help guide each one to a saintly life, in imitation of these patrons. They were asked to report to the class on the results of our research.

The resources for this research were not too abundant: the regular dictionary, *The Catholic Encyclopedia*, Greek and Latin dictionaries, the lives of the saints, and the Bible.

FRATER TOBIAS

Frater Tobias was the first to report. Fellow novices thought it appropriate that he had this name and gave him the nickname, Toby, for he was portly. He proudly stated that he thought that Tobias, nevertheless, was a very strong name. He started his talk with a reference to the *Hebrew Testament* book, *Tobias*. "The name has a great meaning, namely, Yahweh is good," he began.

Among the books found in the recent discovery of five Dead Sea Scrolls was the *Book of Tobias* in both Aramaic and Hebrew. Many think of the book as a romantic novel with a captivating narrative. The father, an Israelite of the Northern Kingdom, is called Tobit and the son, Tobias. The Tobit family has been exiled from their homeland and now live in the Assyrian capital, Nineveh. There, the father provides for the most vulnerable members of society, the widow, orphan, and resident alien. Despite these charitable acts, Tobit suffers a series of misfortunes and sends his son on a journey to retrieve a fortune left behind with a relative.

Tobias arrives at the home of his kinsman, Gabael, to retrieve the family money. Here he meets Sarah, who like the tales of Ali Baba, has seven consecutive husbands who have all died on the night of their wedding. Tobias and Sarah fall in love and marry, but Tobias does not die. There are interesting stories about the demonic possessions of Sarah, the help of the messenger of God, archangel Raphael, and magic potions and venomous bird droppings.

"Just to make my case that my namesake is fantastic; in the library I saw depictions of a set of four beautiful seventeeth-century silk needlework tapestries based on the *Book of Tobias*. Well, Tobias is certainly important for he is one of the characters in Shakespeare's *Twelfth Night*.

"Those with the name can become great peacemakers for they can have excellent diplomatic abilities and can be supportive mediators. While they may be kind of introverts, they can still be personable, compassionate and real charmers," Frater Tobias concluded, alluding, tongue in cheek, to himself.

FRATER CALLISTUS

Frater Callistus gave the second report. His baptismal name was Laverne, but the Abbot decided that upon entering the monastery, he had to change his name to that of a saint. He chose Callistus, a rather unusual name but he found some important facts about this saint.

The name is of Greek and Latin origin and means most beautiful. This was the name of three popes including one from the third century, Callistus I, who is regarded as a saint and is mentioned in the canon of the Mass. And it is also the name of an antipope. Although the name is not too common today, it was the name of many celebrities in the past.

Callistus I was the bishop of Rome, 218 AD to his death in 223. He lived during the reigns of the Roman Emperors Elagabalus and Alexander Severus.

"But we actually don't know much about my patron saint. The most information we have about him is from someone who hated him. Imagine what facts there might be if your biography was written by an enemy of yours! And to add to the conundrum, that enemy, Hippolytus, was a rival candidate for the chair of Peter; he is also regarded as a saint. But whom are we to believe?"

These two saints had opposite philosophies of life. Hippolytus was rigid in his adherence to rules and regulations. The early church had been tough in giving penances to those who committed sins of adultery, murder or fornication. Some theologians held that certain sins were too serious to be forgiven through confession. Hippolytus' catalogue of sins that Callistus allegedly permitted included extramarital sex and early forms of contraception.

So, Hippolytus was enraged at the mercy that Callistus showed these repentant sinners for he allowed them to receive communion again after they had performed public penance. Callistus also affirmed the equality of free people and slaves for he accepted marriages between them. Hippolytus saw in Callistus' mercy a manifestation of submission to lust and licentiousness, reflecting not holiness but perversion and fraud.

Class conscious Hippolytus had additional misgivings about Callistus because he had been a slave. Callistus' past life as allegedly a failed bank manager who embezzled money led to Hippolytus' accusation that Callistus had spent the money on his own pleasure-seeking. According to Hippolytus, Callistus did not face up to his misdeeds but fled in order to escape punishment. Eventually he was brought back to Rome, put on trial and sentenced to cruel punishment–forced labor on a treadmill. After his release, Callistus allegedly disrupted a synagogue by shouting for money. He was arrested, sentenced again, this time sent to the Sardinian mines.

Hippolytus' story does not end here for eventually Pope Zephyrinus recalled Callistus to Rome, part of an amazing, rising and twisted path. He was ordained a deacon and became the caretaker of a major and early Christian Roman cemetery that still bears his name, Cemetery or Catacomb of St. Callistus. He advised and guided the Pope in orthodox theology and was regarded as the power behind the church before he became bishop of Rome.

After Pope Zephyrinus died, Callistus was proclaimed pope over the protests of rival candidate Hippolytus. Again, as Pope Callistus, he chose to mercifully embrace sinners rather than merely judge and dismiss them. He is listed as a martyr (along with Hippolytus) but there is no record of how he was martyred or by whom. Because of one of his occupations, he became the patron saint of undertakers, gravediggers and cemetery workers.

Two wildly opposing views of penitence, a story told by an enemy, a slave and an alleged ex-convict who headed the church. The church was large enough to embrace the perspectives of both Callistus and Hippolytus and proclaim both of them saints.

"I think the name Callistus has a wonderful chic quality," Frater Callistus concluded. "It's appealing and refined; it blends character with flair and there are qualities of Callistus that I want to imitate: he is a practical but compassionate person, shrewd, a leader. In spite of his lowly position and his alleged failings, or because of them, he demonstrated the mercy of Christ to everyone. He forgave because he was forgiven. *Callistus lunatus* is a species of ground beetle, but I am not sure what guidance that can give me!"

FRATER JEROME

Frater Jerome was next to talk about his patron saint. "I found a lot of material on St. Jerome, my patron," Frater Jerome began. "I wasn't supposed to snoop all over the library but I did get into the art section and found in a book an unfinished reproduction of St. Jerome in the Wilderness, painted by Leonardo da Vinci about 1480. This oil sketch was cut into five separate pieces but was eventually put together to form a single whole.

"In da Vinci's painting, Jerome is of advanced age and looks haggard from fasting as a hermit in a dark cave in the Syrian desert. In agony, he kneels in a rocky landscape, his eyes gazing with determination at a crucifix. In his outstretched right hand, he holds a rock and is about to beat his chest in penance. At his feet is a lion, a loyal companion after he extracted a thorn from its paw; with its curled tail, it is now locked in an embrace with Jerome. The lion is a symbol of power associated with the *Gospel of Mark*.

"A thin layer of flesh covers Jerome's bones, the muscles of his cheek, his neck and nearly toothless mouth. In the background is a lake surrounded by precipitous mountains shrouded in mist. I found Leonardo's fingerprints on the paint surface. There are some pointers in this painting that are worthy of imitation."

Jerome lived in the fourth century, was a commentator and translator of the Bible and a learned Latin Father of the Church. For a time, he lived as a hermit, was ordained a priest and served as secretary to Pope Damasus I. He established a monastery at Bethlehem. A wealthy Roman aristocrat, Paula, funded his stay in a cave, amply provided his means of livelihood and helped increase his collection of books. He translated the *Old Testament* from the original Hebrew.

"His commentaries on the Bible, his ascetical, monastic, and theological works greatly influenced the early Middle Ages," Frater Jerome continued. "A doctor of the church, we know him especially for his Latin translation of the Bible, called the *Vulgate*, meaning the current common language. As a continuation of this work, Pope Damasus commissioned him in 382 to provide a serviceable text of the Gospels for the liturgy."

Two events drove him to this feverish activity. The first was in response to his sexual escapades as a student in Rome. He suffered terrible bouts of guilt about this. To salve his conscience, he visited the burial grounds of martyrs and apostles in the catacombs. These experiences reminded him of the terrors of hell that he might merit. As a consequence, he pursued an ascetic life and for a while spent time as a hermit in the desert.

The second event which energized him occurred within a dream during which he was dragged before a law court of the Lord; he was accused of being a Ciceronian, a follower of the first-century B.C. Roman statesman, orator, lawyer and philosopher, Marcus Tullius Cicero, rather than a follower of Christ. For this, in his reverie, he was severely lashed and then vowed not to read or possess pagan literature again.

His family was Christian and fairly wealthy, and Jerome was well educated at home and in Rome, primarily in grammar and rhetoric. Although he described his early life as one of idleness and lack of scholarly ambition, Jerome was a man of extremes. He disciplined his unruly passions through harsh penances and studied Hebrew, although he kind of hated the language. Jerome was one of the pivotal figures in the history of the preservation and transmission of the Bible, a brilliant, temperamental, dedicated, irascible scholar.

"His response to temptation was incessant prayer and fasting. He had a fierce temper and a strong will which he directed in an explosive way against those he considered heretical; he often made enemies, but he emphasized the love of Christ. He once described the heretic Pelagius as the most stupid person whose wits were dulled by too much Scottish porridge!

"In addition to insights into St. Jerome's mind and his age from his writings on cases of conscience and theological elaborations, we get a personal picture of his eating habits. He was a kind of vegetarian, writing about the symptoms and cure of a severe vitamin A deficiency. For a time, he ate only barley bread and vegetables slightly cooked without oil. However, since his eyes were growing dim and his skin became rough, he again added oil to his food.

"He was strong in defense of the perpetual virginity of Mary and of the superiority of the single over the married life. Since he observed signs of the disintegration of Greco-Roman civilization, he expected that the world would soon end.

"His life is associated with a lion but in the late Middle Ages, he is shown either in his study, surrounded by books, or in a rocky desert. Since he considered life rather meaningless and gave scant consideration to earthly goods, he is shown with a skull, and the admonition, *Cogita mori,* think upon death; he is also shown with an image of the last judgment, a candle, an hourglass and a trumpet, also with an image of an owl, a symbol of wisdom and scholarship."

Frater Jerome's presentation was too lengthy for one class, so he continued the next day. For St. Jerome, it made sense that if the Bible was to continue shaping Christian faith and life, it had to be rendered in the current language. He strove to make the translation equivalent to the original not just in meaning but also in quality of style. Any translation should reflect the new language used at its best–this Jerome learned from Cicero.

"Just as Jerome was merciless and abusive toward his opponents, he was gentle and kind toward his friends and the needy. Many people sought his advice on how to live their Christian lives. He founded a school for boys at Bethlehem and served as a spiritual guide for the monks and nuns near him. He gave shelter to refugees who came to the Holy Land following the sack of Rome by the Vandals in 410.

"I found that many quotations from Jerome's works spurred my reflections. He underlined the importance of the Bible:

"'Ignorance of the Scriptures is ignorance of Christ.

"'A man who is well grounded in the testimonies of the Scripture is the bulwark of the Church.'

"Since I have studied piano, I found the following quote insightful: 'Music to me is a voice, my voice, it's my way of expressing what colors can I bring in, what emotions, what I feel. What ideas can I bring out from these instruments that would make this song come alive.'

"He prized virginity above marriage: 'And as regards Adam and Eve, we must maintain that before the fall they were virgins in Paradise, but after they sinned, and were cast out of Paradise, they were immediately married.

"'Woman is the gate of the devil, the road to iniquity, the sting of the scorpion, in a word, a dangerous species.

"'I praise wedlock, I praise marital union, but only because they produce me virgins.'

"And on prayer and fasting: 'To saints their very slumber is a prayer. When the stomach is full, it is easy to talk of fasting. A fat stomach never breeds fine thoughts.

"'There are things in life that are bigger than ourselves. Life is short, live it well.

"'Martyrdom does not consist only in dying for one's faith. It also consists in serving God with love and purity of heart every day of one's life.

"'Always be doing something worthwhile; then the devil will always find you busy.

"'The enemy of reflection is the breakneck pace–the thousand pictures.

"'Nothing is hard for lovers, no labor is difficult for those who wish it.'"

FRATER LEO

Frater Leo was the last presenter. "I chose Pope Leo the Great as my patron. He lived 400–461 AD and was Pope and bishop of Rome from 440–461. He was born into the Roman aristocracy in Tuscany and settled many disputes both religious and secular.

"As a great pastor, he helped with charitable works in Rome. I especially like his Christmas day sermon: 'Let us put off then the old man with his deeds, and having obtained a share in the birth of Christ, let us renounce the works of the flesh. Christian, acknowledge thy dignity, and becoming a partner in the Divine nature, refuse to return to the old baseness by degenerate conduct. Remember the Head and the Body of which thou art a member.' He articulates a dignity common to all Christians, whether saints or sinners, and the obligation to live up to it.

"As Pope, he helped centralize the church and reaffirmed papal authority, with the pope as the chief patriarch of the western church. He was the first to call himself the successor of St. Peter. What is true of St. Peter is true also of his successors. While every bishop has pastoral care of his particular flock, the Roman pontiff has care over the whole church. Other bishops are his assistants in this great task.

"Pope Leo was a heresy killer, working diligently to oppose and root out numerous heresies that were threatening the western church. Among these heresies was Pelagianism which involved denying original sin and failing to understand the necessity of God's grace for salvation. At the foundation of the Pelagian error was the notion that we can perfect ourselves without God's grace and assistance.

"The other major heresy was Manichaeism which denied the goodness of creation, the human body, and even matter itself. It failed to understand the full implications of the Genesis account in which God saw that everything he created was good and human beings were very good. Since the Son of God became human, he made everything holy.

"Some Christians questioned the teaching of the church concerning the relationship between Jesus' humanity and his divinity, and how to articulate this mystery of the Christian faith. In response, Pope Leo resolved the doctrinal controversy with a letter stating the church's official teaching on Jesus Christ as one person with a human and a divine nature that could not be separated. This astute letter reconciled the disputing parties.

"St. Leo also influenced aspects of the church year. He replaced pagan holidays with Christian celebrations and began the practice of fasting during certain church seasons like the Ember days, and linked this practice with charity and almsgiving.

"Not only a spiritual and theological leader, he was also an administrative and secular one. As a peacemaker, he led Rome's successful defense against Attila the Hun's barbarian invasion of Italy in 452. During Rome's decline, and as a pastor, Pope Leo took care of his people by fostering charitable work in areas affected by famine, an influx of refugees, and poverty. After Vandal King Genseric sacked and plundered Rome in 455, Pope Leo met the invader and dissuaded him from killing Roman citizens and burning city buildings. The Basilicas of Saints Peter, Paul and John were spared. He helped to rebuild the city. To him, being a Christian was not only about embracing the fullness of the Gospel but living it out in a world filled with hurt, suffering and needs.

"When my mother heard that I was taking the name of Leo, she ordered and sent me a sterling silver medal of him. The novice master approved my keeping and wearing it. This image has Pope Leo, looking rather old and pensive, seated at a desk in front of a crucifix. Wearing the papal crown, he is writing with a quill pen. An inscription in French around the edge of the medal reads: *Sante Leone P.M. P.P.N.* It means, Holy Leo, Supreme Pontiff, pray for us.

"I will treasure this medal and hope it will help me to be a pontifex in my own way, a bridge-builder. Other images associated with Pope Leo include the Virgin, and a pick axe and horse, suggesting his work at rooting out heresies, but also undertaking down-to-earth tasks, which he did, such as supervising the distribution of grain imports and reorganizing the municipal fire department. His feast day is Nov. 10 in the Roman calendar and Feb. 18 in the Byzantine tradition.

"Pope Leo followed Jesus' advice, be perfect as your heavenly Father is. He was not an elitist, but believed everyone should work at spiritual growth, depend on the grace of God and try to meet the highest standard.

"I had a lot of questions before I entered the monastery as a novice," Frater Leo said. "I was surprised that I was invited to enter in the first place. The Abbot and Father Martin knew of my past and asked: 'Could I forego all that the world offers, close myself off forever within these brick walls, and search for God with a routine way of life?' They referred to Thomas à Kempis who wrote that as often as he went into the world, he came back less a man. And also, to Meister Eckhart who viewed that such detachment helped engage in divine immobility, for God is pure, simple, immutable. Such a detachment is possible, I was told, only if one is empty of creatures, full of God, for if one is full of creatures, one is empty of God.

"In my preliminary meeting with Father Martin, he stated that my perfection has to be tailored to myself and my abilities and should not be the same as anyone else. He noted that Benedictines are not powerful and privileged but are supposed to be humble, work on the nitty gritty of spiritual growth, step by step. We are dependent on the grace of God even if we do not seem to grow in holiness. We are not failures even if we do not meet the highest standard. But, nevertheless, it is good to go after your highest dreams and push the boundaries."

"While there is suffering and pain in Christian life, a circle of thorns, much toil and effort and seldom a positive result," the novice master said, "there is joy in being with brothers sharing the same expectations, joy in peace, joy in simple food."

"I accepted what he said even though a lot of it was confusing to me."

Reading

ONE OF THE MONKS read in the dining room/refectory at the noon and evening meals. The reading part of the meal began with a request from the reader for a blessing of the superior, followed by a short passage from the Bible and then the main reading. The superior occasionally interrupted this procedure during a festive occasion or when there was a special guest. Then the superior rang his bell and monks replied with *Deo gratias,* Thanks be to God! Talking and sharing ensued. A passage from the Rule always concluded the meal.

Some of the novices were surprised by the selection of readings. There were many readings from the Jesuit *Relations,* those reports that the Jesuits sent home to France during their seventeenth-century missionary activities largely in New France. It was understandable that the Abbot would select passages from history in general since that was his training and presumably his delight. Accounts of murder, however, and the Jesuits' taking care of their bathroom (without a bathroom) necessities did not seem appropriate for wholesome eating and digestion! One of the readers had a different approach to injudicious or unsavory passages. His changes were understandable for he had served as an aide in the Canadian diplomatic corps. "There are several sections here," he noted, "one of which is pertinent." He didn't need the Abbot to tell him exactly what to read.

Then there was the reading of a lengthy tome by J. Edgar Hoover, *Masters of Deceit, The Story of Communism in America and How to Fight It.* Again, it fit into the theme of historical perspectives but some monks silently disapproved: "Did we have to hear in great detail about the mostly alleged affairs of the Communists in the United States, those Trojan horses? How did Hoover's rightist position fit into the policies of the socialist government in Saskatchewan and with the slightly left-leaning and human-ist positions of the monastic paper and its concern for the average working person? And it is such a lengthy book." The novices overheard other critical comments of the book. One noted that this book should, in fairness, by followed by a reading of *The Communist Manifesto* by Karl Marx and something by Friedrich Engels. Another monk thought that, while there were Communist influences in the American past, this was largely fear-mongering now. "We can't peg all problems such as marital ones on the influence of pinkoes," an elderly monk commented. "The idea of sharing wealth and guaranteeing basic so-cial services are not horrible ideas. Jazz music was not a result of Commu-nist influence." While some monks thought this reading was a good history of Communism, another would give it five stars if it were read as comedy but zero stars if it was taken seriously.

Another book selected for monastic reading was *Silent Spring* by Rachel Carson; this selection was surprising for it was in contrast to the Hoover one and gave a perspective on the proper care of nature that many considered embodied in the Rule. Also, *Silent Spring* was a scientific study by a woman who in some way was now speaking in the monastery. When she wrote of the use of the insecticide DDT causing damage to wildlife, agricultural animals and even humans, some monks thought she was ad-dressing them, for their farm was using herbicides and pesticides, 2,4-D and 2,4,5-T!

Most readers adhered to the texts as given, but, again, a few were quite flexible. These monks emphasized certain passages, mispronounced words, or deleted sections of the prescribed reading. The Brothers did not read nor did the novices; one monk read the second chapter of the Rule, What the abbot should be like, with the emphasis on *should,* much to the irritation of the Abbot who visibly shuffled his feet under his table and glared at the reader. On another occasion, a monk read the title of a later chapter in the Rule, Monks who do not go very far, stopping to emphasize his point that there were some who indeed did not go very far because were not very gifted.

The novices thought that the Rule embodied a lot of good sense, was moderate in its emphasis on keeping monastic prescriptions and meting out punishments. So, Frater Tobias thought that his sister might also be enamored with the Rule; to this end, he gave her a copy to read. The only feedback she gave was that Benedict was rather harsh in meting out punishments to offenders.

In addition to the more senior monks, those studying for the priesthood were also readers. While the errors committed were not frequent, I recall a few. One of the philosophy students was reading in the refectory during noon and evening meals. He was reading a commentary on Benedictine life by a notable canon lawyer from Rome. He referred to him as Benno Gut, like the gut of one's intestines. All of those eating in silence broke into hilarious and spontaneous laughter, for most of them had used Benno Gut's extensive Latin commentary on canon law and knew that his name was pronounced Goot, the German way, and not gut, the anatomical way. The poor neophyte did not know what was so funny.

On another occasion in the refectory, the reading was from St. Therese Lisieux's autobiography, *The Story of a Soul,* and in it she referred to her sister Celine. The young reader pronounced her name as sea lion which gave rise to puzzling looks. The monk who was appointed to correct the readers sent him a note indicating the correct pronunciation. However, the reader ignored the note and continued with sea lion, much to the annoyance of the corrector. After dinner, and when all the monks had left, the reader was confronted about the mispronunciation and the repudiation of the note. "Oh, I always ignore such notes," the monk responded, not ingratiating him to the corrector! But no punishment was forthcoming.

A few monks broke into titters as a reader read brassiere for brazier and another pronounced the name of a fellow monk, Ildephone, as Idle-phonse.

The readers read for an entire week or part of a week. The Abbot gave a public blessing at the beginning of the week for these readers, sometimes referred to as weakly! readers. In addition to this abbatial blessing, there was another blessing in the monks' dining room just before the reader started. Of course, the reader prepared both in the study hall and then had a trial run in the refectory before the monks processed in for their meals.

Preceding the monks' arrival, the reader went to the podium, put the microphone harness over his head and waited for all of the monks to be seated in their places; the reader then bowed down, asked the Abbot for a blessing, *Jube Domne, benedicere,* Pray Lord, a blessing. Then, just before the Abbot gave the blessing, the reader turned the microphone on. Generally, things went smoothly, but this time the speaker system started fulminating with crackling and sputtering noises. For the reader it was a startling experience and he did not know what to do. The interference continued for what seemed an eternity with the reader quite helpless. The monks did not know what was going on. Finally, the sound quietened, the Abbot gave the blessing, and the reader began with a reading from the *Gospel of John*, "Do not let your hearts be troubled. Believe in God, believe in me." Great laughter followed this appropriate juxtaposition of words, but the reader was perplexed, wondering what he had done wrong again to precipitate this jocularity. Nevertheless, he continued the reading without further incident.

Another young monk was reading the *Song of Songs* in the dining room. He was very nervous but tried to place the proper emphasis on the words and phrases in this emotional text. In fact, one could hear his heavy breathing as he read to his fellow celibates: "How beautiful you are, my love, how beautiful you are! Your eyes, behind your veil, are doves; your hair is like a flock of goats frisking down the slopes of Gilead. Your teeth are like a flock of shorn ewes, as they come up from the washing. Your lips are a scarlet thread and your words enchanting. Your two breasts are two fawns, twins of a gazelle that feed along the lilies." Many monks shivered at this sensuous rendering.

We later learned in our bible class that the *Song of Songs* had a checkered history but remained in the Bible, at least in the Catholic one. Some critics thought it should be expunged for it was way too sensuous and it did not mention God at all. But there it was, proclaimed in the monks' dining room in a sexy manner, making some rather uncomfortable.

One afternoon, Father Martin sauntered into the novitiate quarters and asked us what we were reading. We told him with great pride and for his edification that we were reading the *Gospel of St. John* and in addition a commentary on it in Latin by St. Augustine of Hippo.

He did not want to add to our obvious pride and so diffused the conversation somewhat. He told us a story about an occasion in the dining room of a large monastery when all the monks were eating their noon meal. This room was in the basement with huge open windows to let in the breezy air on this hot summer day.

For his penance, one of the mischievous novices was kneeling before the Abbot's dining room table for he always had a witty saying about every situation and was being punished for being so smart-assed. Suddenly a donkey put his head through one of the open windows and gave a loud hee haw into the quarters. The usual table reading was interrupted as all the monks, including, unusually, the Abbot, erupted in loud bursts of laughter.

After the uproar subsided, the Abbot, still in a jovial mood, asked the aberrant novice whether he had an apt saying to cover the situation and that saying might then absolve him of punishment for his present misdemeanor. The monk wittily replied, quoting *St. John's Gospel:* "He came unto his own and his own received him not!" Father Martin could not remember whether the monks engaged in further laughter or whether they took St. John's words as a scolding and as a fitting reply by the donkey.

Monastic garb: the habit

THE ABBOT OF THE monastery had two criteria in assigning new names to or retaining present ones for the novices: one criterion was that the name had to be that of a saint and the second was that it could not be the same as any member of the community.

Novices were invested with monastic clothing, generally called a habit. They were instructed to say an individualized prayer when donning its various parts: a long, black, ankle-length flowing garment, a cassock, buttoned in the front, donned with the accompanying prayer in Latin, "Clothe me with the new man of justice and truth;" a scapular (originally a front-to-back work apron the width of the shoulders). After kissing it, the monk prayed, "Lord who said, 'my yoke is sweet and my burden light,' make it so that as I wear this scapular I may merit your grace;" a belt, a symbol of chastity, (leather, then cloth for those who made vows); a cloth collar to be superseded by a plastic white collar for those in vows, and, lastly, a hood, a necessity while living and praying in cold monasteries. This cowl or hood was pulled over the head during prayers, beginning on the colder days in Advent and continuing throughout Lent and winter. "It made sense to preserve body heat on those days long ago, but at the present time monks still use the cowl during these times, mostly as a preservation of the ancient ritual," Father Martin said.

"I am still memorizing the prayers when putting on and kissing the various parts of the habit," Frater Jerome said, "The belt involves praying to be girded with justice and purity; the scapular prayer recalls the yoke of Christ."

"Some monks wear the habit when outside the monastery, but most wear a black suit," Father Martin said. "Although the habit was the ordinary garb of the day in Benedict's time, there is discussion about what should be the appropriate clothing for monks today. Should we shorten the cassock to be modern? Regular clothing is worn during outside work times."

"I notice that I am wearing more than I usually do on this hot July day," Frater Leo recalled. "In addition to my t-shirt and pants, I have this long garb that goes down to the floor, and the scapular and hood. My neck is crimped up with that cloth band." "Although air can flow through these garments, I am already sweating," Frater Callistus said.

"And a joke about the habit," Father Martin interjected: "We will have a year of bad habits!"

Upon making final, solemn or perpetual vows, monks received a cuculla, a long, flowing black hooded and pleated garment, with wide sleeves worn over the ordinary habit. The cuculla was used on special occasions: feast of St. Michael the Archangel, and various solemnities, Christmas and Easter.

With the names and garments in place, the acting novice master indicated that the novices would be addressed by the title Frater, meaning brother, distinguishing them ambiguously from those who were in the monastery but were not destined for ordination; these were called in English, Brother. Those who were ordained were called Father, or, in formal terms, Reverend.

Work is prayer, prayer is work

LATER THAT DAY, FATHER Martin addressed the issue of work. In his Rule, St. Benedict writes that "idleness is the devil's workshop." In this chapter he outlines a rather precise daily schedule that includes time for manual labor. If some monks have difficulty filling their Sundays with reading, they should be given light work. His attitude toward work is that monks should be kept busy for if they don't work, they might get into trouble.

According to St. Benedict they are real monks when they live by the labor of their hands. There is legitimate pride in accomplishment, in self-sufficiency. But St. Benedict is not the patron saint of work for its own sake; he does not think that life is work. Here, the motto, *ora et labora* fits in: pray and work. Prayer is very important, one of the goals, the eminent one, for monks. Added to prayer and work is *lectio divina*, holy reading.

GREGORIAN CHANT

Father Martin gave a talk to us about the Divine Office and Gregorian chant. He pointed to the recitation of the Office but also to the singing. Singing has been a part of Jewish and Christian liturgy for a long time. In his *Letter to the Ephesians*, St. Paul mentions singing and in one of the Gospels, Matthew writes: "After psalms had been sung, they left for the Mount of Olives." One of the early and very short prayers, *Amen*, is found in Jewish, Christian, and Muslim worship as a concluding word or as a response to prayers. *Amen* is often translated as verily or truly; we commonly say So be it, or, when we strongly agree with something, we say I'll add my *Amen* to that.

Another short prayer, *Alleluia*, Praise Yahweh/God, also occurs frequently. Another prayer, the threefold *Sanctus* (Holy) comes from the

Hebrew word, *kadosh,* as in the *Prophet Isaiah,* "Holy, holy, holy is Yahweh Sabaoth, his glory fills the whole earth." The word holy is the Hebrew designation for God, meaning someone/something set apart from the common, singular, awe-inspiring and without rival. God is apart, yet the whole earth is full of his glory.

The longer prayerful songs are sung as Gregorian chant, or plainchant, monophonic, that is, without accompaniment. This chant, although attributed to Pope Gregory the Great in the sixth century, actually developed in western and central Europe during the ninth and tenth centuries.

A book, called the *Graduale* contains the chants or songs for the Mass, together with the Responsorial Psalm after the readings; the book, *Antiphonale,* contains thematic antiphons or verses sung or recited before or after a psalm or canticle for the Divine Office. A canticle is a hymn or chant, often with a biblical text. One of the challenges is to deliver the meaning of words with the chant.

ARSIS AND THESIS

Father Norbert tried to teach us novices how to sing Gregorian chant so that we were not always off pitch/key and were able to stay together. The notes on the page were lifeless in themselves, he said, and we were to give them a musical expression.

He introduced the idea of dynamic contrasts, areas of a piece that are louder or softer than others, for Gregorian chant is a continuous stream of swelling and diminishing musical notes. Ideally, our singing was to be a movement, a state of flux, growing and fading in intensity. Father Norbert called this growth, *arsis;* the fading or diminishing he called *thesis.* Generally, we were to grow and fade with the rising and falling of the notes.

There was another aspect which we did not fully understand: some series of notes or clusters were to be sung lighter than others. The chant director indicated this dynamic; he asked us to begin with an *arsis* and end with a *thesis* and consider seriously the words that we were singing. Above all, "sing with feeling," Father Norbert indicated, raising his frail hands and arms. This feeling was necessary especially in the morning for sleepy monks because there might be a tendency to chant in a monotonous way thinking that no note was more important than another.

"Keeping *arsis* and *thesis* in mind will enhance the beauty of the chant for then the chant's radiance will not be imprisoned in the four-line staff and black and white notes," Father Norbert emphasized.

So, we tried to apply the *arsis and thesis* stuff to the Gregorian notes. "In the Latin, *Viri Galilei*, Men of Galilee, the antiphon for Ascension Thursday, you should love the ascending fourth as you ripple up and soar into the last syllable. Try to stay on pitch; to do so, I might have to use an organ accompaniment especially in the morning."

Father Norbert was a very serious monk hardly ever including a humorous incident, but as he concluded his instruction, he recounted: "One of my novices last year said, 'I always wanted to be a Gregorian monk, but I never got the chants.'"

"I liked Father Norbert's bit of concluding humor," Father Jerome said at recreation time. "That music is enchanting; it has a heavenly quality and yet is rooted in where we are. It is like eating *Stilton* cheese, tangy but also nourishing. It is good but you always want more."

LECTIO DIVINA, SPIRITUAL READING

In the novitiate we had no newspapers except the weekly Saskatchewan *Prairie Messenger*, no radio or television. The novices gathered in chapel, 15 to 20 minutes before the noon prayer of Sext, the sixth hour, for a silent time of spiritual reading and meditation.

Father Martin called this time, *lectio divina*, spiritual/divine reading, a time given exclusively to God, to holy thoughts, to letting him speak. To center one's thoughts he advised novices to read slowly one or more optional texts. One possible text was the *Hebrew Testament*, specifically the psalms for they contained a range of human emotions. One could focus on sections of the *New Testament*. The lives of the saints were good too. He recommended especially *The Imitation of Christ* by Thomas à Kempis; in it he states, as mentioned earlier, that as often as he went into the world, he came back less a man. Well, here we were, kind of out of the world, and trying to reclaim our humanity.

"There should be no hurry, no need to rush through many pages, but instead try to instill a period of calm," Father Martin advised. We were to let the words wash over ourselves, whatever that meant. It was to be a restful time and some took this literally, for rest or sleep came quite naturally. But even this somnolent meditation was not a waste of time, for we learned that St. Teresa of Avila approved it.

Some directives for this meditation were negative: don't try too hard to pray; make peace with unmonastic desires; don't be overly concerned about what other monks think; avoid self-absorption, excessive concern for one's body, and imaginary ills and slights; don't think that engaging in meditation will make you greater or better than anyone else.

Empty yourself of social routines and conventions. If you are not attentive to God, other desires will surface. Our former selves and desires lurk in the background, always waiting to break through their new monastic identity. Letters from home, eagerly awaited, are a double-edged sword; on the one hand, they connect us to people and events we hold dear, but, on the other hand, they can fix us to the past and in this sense they are dangerous. "I can certainly relate to that," Frater Leo thought, "I remember dancing with my girlfriend, playing hockey, and smoking. I am still excited about this freedom and find it extremely hard to suppress my non-spiritual desires."

"Try to center one's thoughts on holy things." Father Martin advised. This was easier said than done for how do you chase out your anxieties, your residual cares about family life, your monastic irritations?

But he also gave some positive directives: make the most of every small insight to grow as a human being; above all, realize that the monastic life is a pearl of great price and Jesus asks us to seek it: "The kingdom of heaven is like a merchant seeking good pearls, who when he had found one of great price, gave all that he had and bought it." Remember that since there is a God, it is important to seek a relationship with him. He is at work in all things, persons and events.

In addition to advice on reading and meditating during this period, Father Martin challenged novices to do other extensive readings during their one-year novitiate. We could read all of the sacred writings, that is, both the *Old* and the *New Testaments*, from beginning to end, even the very dry parts, the chronologies! We would have to allot time and make much effort to do so. We could exclude the psalms, for we would be praying all 150 of them each week. We did not have to read the Rule for it would be read three times during the year, with a chapter after each noon meal.

He then gave a general directive to our lives: *respice, aspice,* and *prospice.* The first one which he had previously downplayed was *respice,* survey your past. What can you learn from it? Then, *aspice,* look around you now.

41

What do you see, what are you experiencing? Then, *prospice:* What is your future? What are you planning to do with your life? What direction are you going?

All of this sounded like great stuff. And I liked the Latin rhythms of *respice, aspice* and *prospice.*

FOOD AND DRINK

St. Benedict writes that while some religious writers prescribe that monks should not have any alcoholic drinks, he makes a concession that since monks in his day cannot be convinced of this, they should drink in moderation and no more than a half bottle a day. He was indeed a man for all seasons. But half a bottle sounds like a lot.

At the abbey, portly Brother Bonaventure was in charge of making wine, using grapes, stomping them, pressing and fermenting them in the process. He saved the best wine from the first pressing for Mass, while the second pressing was served at table on special occasions.

Like all good wine-makers, Brother Bonny, as he was affectionately known, had to taste his creation at specific times in the process. Some monks thought he must have done more than merely taste it, judging from his rotundity. The Abbot became aware of this more than occasional dipping, so he invited him into his room to discuss the direction that the whole winemaking process might take in the future.

Brother Bonny was getting older and monks suggested that the abbey cease winemaking and purchase commercial products. Brother Bonny assured the Abbot that he was willing to continue as winemaker as long as his health permitted. Father Abbot adverted to his heavy weight, noting that this was not good for his longevity; he suggested that he recite the Our Father or several of them when he was tempted to imbibe too much. While reciting it, the Abbot thought, Brother Bonny would not be imbibing.

Brother Bonny agreed to this suggestion, but in the wine cellar he had a mental reservation about it. "I know what I will do, it's the same as we do during our community prayers: the leader announces the Our Father which is followed by a pause so that individuals can say it mentally in silence. In this way, I can both say the Our Father and drink during the pause."

Another monk, Brother Justus, was the head huncho in the carpenter shop. "I remember when I was a student, we used to visit him there," Frater Tobias recalled. "He was very jovial and welcoming. We came to visit him because we wanted to repair our hockey sticks. This was a necessity for me because I had so little money to purchase new ones. He quickly showed us where there was some wood and glue and we could do it ourselves. We found out that since he was a jack-of-all trades, he frequently did repair work for residents in the area. They wanted to pay him in cash for his services, but he insisted they bring him beer and snuff instead. So, he always had an ample supply for afternoon refreshments. Unfortunately, we paid him with a mere thank you."

The Sisters of St. Elizabeth prepared and served the food both in the monastery and in the boys' boarding school. In the morning, mostly oatmeal porridge with rich, whole milk from the farm's dairy herd. In the monastery, bowls for porridge were on our plates and as we sat down, we routinely and quickly dished the oatmeal into them. This unreflective approach caught Frater Leo by surprise, for on this morning there was no bowl on the plates and so he mechanically piled the oatmeal on the empty plate. He watched as fellow novices mechanically made the same mistake.

We mixed butter churned in the kitchen with honey from the apiary to make a smooth and delicious combination. Bread from the oven was always yummy and fresh. Meat from the beef herd and potatoes and other vegetables comprised the noon and evening meals. Especially notable were the succulent tomatoes. Desserts of various kinds were cakes and cookies, and rhubarb, saskatoon, and pumpkin pies.

In season fruits were crab apples, raspberries and strawberries from the orchard and garden and commercial fruit the Sisters canned in the fall. For most of us the fare was like that of our home farms except there we had morning and afternoon snacks and the occasional store-bought goodies. A rare treat in the monastery was the serving of roasted pigeons procured from the abbey barns, one for each monk.

In the winter the outdoor skating rink had two dressing shacks, one for the visiting hockey team and the other for the home one. In early fall, these shacks housed many pailfuls of tomatoes that the novices and others had picked. Every other day, novices would sort them into pails, one for ripened ones, one for rotten and over ripened, and one for green ones. Frater Tobias took glee in finding the rotten ones and threw them with great force into the designated pail, often hitting the rim or missing it altogether; it made a great splat and scattered over the parkas of unsuspecting fellow novices.

This was a time to do a lot of talking and Frater Leo filled the silence. "I know I should have thrown away a card I had for some time," he said.

"But I have it on me and I would like to share it with you. It's kind of fun, a Turtle's Club card I sort of earned some time ago. To become a member, you have to answer four questions, and here they are; see how you do. They might seem provocative, but you have to answer beyond the first and obvious thing that comes into your mind.

"The first question to become a member of the Ancient and Honorable Order of Turtles is: What is it a man can do standing up, a woman sitting down and a dog on three legs? Regardless of what you think, the correct answer is shake hands! Second question: What is it that a cow has four of and a woman has only two of? The correct answer is legs. Third question: What is a four-letter word ending in K that means the same as intercourse? Correct answer is talk. Last question: What is it on a man that is round, hard and sticks so far out of his pajamas that you can hang a hat on it? Correct answer is head. Your answers indicate whether you have the highest morals and good character. If you answered the riddles correctly, you are welcome to become a member of the pure-minded Order of Turtles! Membership benefits charities of your choice."

"I needed some coaching to get the answers right," Frater Jerome confessed.

The monks, Sisters and hired staff provided most of the food for themselves and their students. Monks believed that what we eat determines what we become. Without much self-reflection, monks cared for their land and were regarded by the university as a setting for agricultural days, for experimenting with new equipment and agricultural products.

There was great satisfaction in being nearly self-sufficient. And it was economical to do so, from employing bees to make honey, to growing a large garden and orchard, to raising wheat for sale and oats for animals, to producing meat and milk, to eating on occasion the barns' plentiful pigeons. There was joy in living and sharing in the wonders of nature. Knowing where their food came from connected them to nature and the world, and was nutritious.

Ordinarily the novices did not enter the monastery's lunch room. Its walls were plain and its fare spartan, with a refrigerator containing milk and a few cookies. Obviously, the coffee maker had not taken a vow of silence, but the not-so-solemn assortment of characters broke the leaden silence not often with golden but at least with bronze conversation. It was a place for informal association, a time to banter about, a time away from regular tasks. It was a scene of some tensions also, as a fellow monk told me. On at least one occasion, a monk punched another in the face and also scraped his dirty shoe on a fellow monk's pants.

SILENCE

During our prayer time in the chapel, it was sometimes unbelievably quiet. No outside noises except an occasional airplane overhead. No noisy breathing and hardly a perceptible sound except for the turning of a page. Then a loud burst of sound. Oh no, Frater Leo was farting again. We pretended not to notice in secret nervousness. This should not happen in the chapel and should not cause an interruption in our sacred meditation!

We cast furtive glances to make sure it was Frater Leo. Our eyes crossed in a mixture of inappropriateness, embarrassment and giggling. But we should have been somewhat acclimatized to this outburst for he had done it unashamedly before. He just felt uneasy under pressure and the release seemed to be in character. No overt embarrassment at all. Hopefully it was a dry and not a wet one.

Those of us from a rural setting were used to a relatively silent world, even though there were varied sounds, interruptions and animal and human crepitation. Although at times of seeding grain and harvesting it, there was a clamoring to get the jobs done, other times were uneventful. The roar of a train in the distance, cars on the road, the mooing of cows and the oinking of pigs but that was within a predictable atmosphere.

There were tasks which had their regimen and rhythm: getting up in the morning and making a fire, going outside to do the chores, hitching the horse and going to school, driving a tractor with its constant and loud purring. These were tasks which made its demands but at a relatively slow pace, with little agitation and relative quiet. I could bond with the animals and the land in such protracted periods of silence. I could think and sing.

The topic of silence and laughter had come up before and this time Father Martin thought he should bring in a little levity to this very serious topic: "An old friend of the Abbot visited him and during supper time silence prevailed until one monk stood up and said, 'sixteen.' All the monks laughed heartily and then resumed their silent meal. Then another monk stood up and said, 'thirty-two' and all the monks burst into gales of laughter.

"The guest was puzzled and asked the Abbot quietly, 'I don't understand why everyone laughs when someone says a number.'

"Well," the Abbot said, "all of us love jokes. In this intimate community all of the monks know these jokes very well and to save time we gave each one of them a number. So, if a monk says a number, all of us remember the relevant joke."

"Can I have a go at this?" the guest asked. The Abbot said that that would be fine.

"So, the visitor stood up and said, 'twenty-four.' But no one laughed. The monks stared at him and then continued their meal.

"I don't understand why no one laughed when I said 'twenty-four.'"

"I don't know," the Abbot responded, "but perhaps it's the way you tell 'em."

"Apologies for that joke," Father Martin said, "but it is actually from my brother, and he was called the punster from Muenster."

"I was not used to prolonged periods of silence," Frater Tobias interjected, "for there was chatter in the recess period at school, during the fall/fowl suppers, and during Sunday visits with relatives."

What to make of this silence, relative or absolute? It seemed like nothing, nothing tangible, nothing really real. It was an absence almost like air, an absence which is also a presence. Is silence like God, not something, not a characteristic, more like nothing, but still a presence that is hard if not impossible to describe?

Father Martin threw out a quote from the philosopher, Soren Kierkegaard that life is meant to be lived forward but can only be understood backward.

"I found this quote quite challenging, a little out of context, but also perplexing," Frater Tobias said later.

To achieve a closeness with God? Again, easier said than done. And is it possible to measure such a closeness which is not a physical closeness or distance? The process seems demanding and severe. "But monks are dumb," a savant wrote, "and so they attempt it." Is it more a process of overcoming one's own demons? How does one dim one's ego and even love those who irritate one? It's like climbing Mount Everest, a spiritual marathon. But there is something seductive in the process. One has to confirm that monastic life and this process is not everyone's cup of tea but might still be a glass of wine.

Father Martin recommended that we read Thomas Merton's *Seven Storey Mountain*. We suspected he recommended it mostly because he was reading it and was enamored with Merton's romantic style. He noted the following for our meditation: Merton mused that the key difference between monks and the rest of mankind is that monks can choose their own battleground upon which to fight the devil. After all, they entered the monastery of their own free will and others outside the monastery do not necessarily have such choices.

SPILLING THE BEANS

A telephone call came from the parents of one of the Brothers that they had a superabundance of green beans. Because the beans were scarce in the monks' garden and because they were deemed a necessary vegetable for the table, Father Martin rallied the novices to take the station wagon and pick beans for the monks' and students' larder. He procured the keys to the newly purchased vehicle, loaded it with bags, basins and pails and we were on our way, with Brother Gregory coming along to help in the picking.

The novice master was not a skilled driver, for he, although of middle age, had earned his driver's license only this year. To add to the challenge, it had rained a lot overnight and the forecast was for more rain. Travel was over muddy and gravel roads, but the troupe of garden harvesters arrived at the farm in good shape in mid-morning.

"I could not believe the rapid-fire conversation that Brother Gregory and the host mother had. She had such a high-pitched voice and gave Brother a lot for his money," Frater Callistus noted.

In a few hours, the garden beans were picked and everyone packed into the station wagon for the journey home. Father Martin was less than cautious as he sped along the slippery road and started veering from one side to the other, sliding off the shoulder and tipping the vehicle. The glass shattered on its side and the roof caved in. No one was injured and a passing farmer packed the bean pickers into his vehicle and took them back to the abbey.

In the Chapter of Faults later that week, Father Martin confessed: "I was a careless driver and I spilled the beans!" In this context, Father Martin spoke to the novices about this kind of semi-public examination. "Here the monks in vows confess their faults in front of their peers. The confession can be quite general and is taken from a formula, a list in Latin. But one can get specific as I did.

"In the past, a monk could confess on others, showing how this monk was unChristlike. In the past, also, some physical discipline was prescribed or taken on voluntarily, such as using a flail on exposed skin, a discipline for the mortification of the flesh, especially for sexual fantasies. Today, we do not go to such extremes, thinking that living out daily tasks well is sufficient penance. But even in its mild present form of public confession, our egos can be ground down quickly.

"Others confessed faults such as snooping in stores for little items, faults against poverty by using a little money for personal gratification, peccadillos like the ones a monk had committed while a student; faults against charity such as disgust for others' errors, being impatient, not passing food, making patronizing comments, remarks about laggards; being late for choir; showing ambition, doing things to compete, stating views too strongly; not preparing well for Office, classes. Not admitting wrong, arguing to assert oneself, having a superior attitude, questioning acts of a superior, disrespectful remarks; faults about not keeping custody of the eyes, little care for equipment, breaking things, tearing one's habit through carelessness, not washing properly; wasting food; overeating."

OTHER WORK PROJECTS

It was important for the novices to get outside of the monastic building, to breathe some fresh air, to pursue legitimate diversions, to get some exercise. Although the Rule's command for novices was only threefold–eat, sleep, and pray–there were ample instructions to engage in manual labor.

Father Martin extended St. Benedict's threefold instruction to include trimming the concentric hedges and cedars around the monastic cemetery. The novices were provided with clippers and stepladders to do that job. They were instructed not to clip too deeply into the hedges but to give them a neat, rounded look. One novice gave in to his fervor to clip well and made a significant gouge in the grove. When the novice master surveyed the work, he noticed the hole and lashed out at the unnamed and overzealous culprit. The novices maintained solidarity in not naming the victim, much to the dismay of the master.

Winter work was involving and challenging. We had to don long underwear bundle up and wear a warm parka, a scarf, mitts, a toque, woolen stockings and felt boots. Only then were we were ready to brave the cold.

The novices regarded work as leading to results for they regarded the work ethic as meaningful; however, they found this was not always the case in the monastery. So, when we were given axes to cut down trees in winter time, we showed our diligence: cutting them near the ground, trimming off the branches and putting them in neat piles and stacking the logs in symmetrical rows.

The master obviously did not have such a seriousness about the results in mind, but envisioned this activity as merely fulfilling the need for fresh air and a respite. Consequently, in the spring the farm boss summarily burned the piles of branches and also the carefully stacked logs in order to clear the land for breaking and cultivation.

One casualty in the jovial axe-cutting enterprise was that Frater Leo, not the most dexterous, wielded his axe in too haphazard a manner, trimming off many branches but also cutting his big toe. Fellow monks helped him hobble to a monastic make-shift clinic for a bandage and then to the nearby hospital for stitches.

GARDENING

An extensive garden was necessary to feed the monks and the boarding students. In early spring, the head of gardening had already planted seeds for tomatoes in his many hotbeds. After the seeds had sprouted into seedlings, he requested that the novices help him transplant these early plants into the garden. He did not want to do this operation too early in the season, however, since there might be a late frost which would stunt these fledgling plants and deprive the monks and college students of healthy tomatoes. This head gardener reminded everyone that these tender shoots would barely survive an early frost.

"I never transplanted them before June 6, for a frost before this time might kill them. But the weather forecast indicates that frost will not occur on this morning," he stated.

Heeding the scientific rather than past wisdom, and trusting the relatively warm weather, he instructed the novices to transplant the seedlings early. After the day-long laborious transplanting, he still felt uneasy about this very early process. Consequently, he monitored the temperatures after midnight and found them dropping precipitously.

At 4 am, he hurried to don his work clothes and drove the garden's tractor with its water tank and pump to the transplanted area; he proceeded to spray the tender sprouts, hoping to dispel the frost's sting. But his attempt to dissipate the freezing with sprays of water was largely to no avail.

They froze, they wilted and turned black. In the late morning, so as not to lose the seedlings, all novices were on deck to lift the plants slightly from their habitation in the soil and then pack the ground around them. The seedlings were a little stunted but since there was no subsequent frost, they grew into healthy tomato plants. The lesson: trust past wisdom and not the so-called scientific weather forecast!

During the fall, novices were assigned to the abbey orchard in the morning to pick apples until noon. The custodian of the orchard, August, generally worked in the piggery, but also trimmed the orchard trees. At this time, he was picking apples for canning, juicing, making jams and jellies and for general eating. August took great pride in keeping the orchard in good condition and was knowledgeable about all the trees and fruit shrubs. He told the novices that the ancient name for apple was *malus* in Latin. *Malus* also meant evil and so it has a great carryover from the Garden of Eden account where the first parents reputedly ate the apple, *malus*, that is also evil, *malus*.

Frater Leo responded to the sun's soothing rays and took off his shirt, baring his hairy chest. "I like to get a sun tan for it is very healthy. I don't use a cap and brown my face and forehead. Most farmers use hats or caps and so they show a shading on their foreheads, the lower part, very bronze, and the upper part white. I call it a farmer line."

Novices were told to begin picking the Rescue apple because its whitish flesh is relatively soft and so is good for immediate eating and canning. "Rescues are small and dull red and are best picked when they are slightly under ripe for they become mushy when fully ripe," August said. "So, they should be used right away. And they are also good for jelly. This apple was introduced in 1933 by the Agricultural Research Station in Scott, Saskatchewan," August informed the novices with pride.

August liked the Adam apple trees the best; their new leaves are a red tint in spring, turn green in the summer and become a beautiful orange-red in the fall. Small, glossy, red fruit on the outside with blood red pulp inside follow the pink flowers; they remain on the branches into the winter providing food for the birds. "The trees are quite tall," August said, "and require a stepladder to reach their uppermost branches. They are disease resistant and can take a lot of frost.

"I will take you to the Hyer Number 12 trees. I like them for the quality and size of the apples. They produce a lot of yellow green fruit which is good for eating and cooking. They keep well when picked green and are very hardy and drought resistant. I forget where they originated in Saskatchewan, Melville or Neville, in 1940.

"I don't prune the crabapple trees very much at all. I saw off dead branches so that disease doesn't get a hold of them. I try and do it in the early spring before the leaves appear, although I hope I don't cut off the live branches. To prevent this, I scratch the branch and remove a little bark; if the flesh is white-green, the branch is alive; if it is brown or black, the branch is dead.

"I try to cultivate around the trees to remove weeds and suckers, but sometimes I need shears to cut them. I am glad that the novices can help both with picking the crabs and also with hoeing the weeds.

"We will pick a lot of crabs for eating and canning. We will use some of them also for juicing, but a lot of them will fall to the ground. Maybe later in the fall, some of you can come and pick them up and do some more juicing," August observed.

August came to the love of these apples honestly. He told us that his father grew apples trees on their farm in Germany. As the present custodian, he said he followed a kind of ritual when he ate apples. He took an apple in his large hands, felt it with his fingers, discerning whether it was hard or soft, rough or smooth. He then eyed the apple all around, and smelled its aroma before gently sinking his teeth into it.

"I remember eating wild raspberries near the horse barns at our parish," Frater Tobias said. "They were small but were they ever good! When we had a break in catechism classes, we immediately went there."

There were raspberry bushes in the abbey orchard also. "As you can see, they are bright red, juicy, have a wonderful smell, are somewhat tart but can be easily separated from the stalks," August noted. "They are great for topping on ice cream or for making wine.

"We have two types of currants in this orchard," August continued. "The Red Currant is a short shrub that sheds its leaves in the fall. As you can see, there are five parts to its bright red berries and maple-like leaves. It is excellent for jams and sauces. Actually, it is related to the gooseberry family and to wild currants.

"The other type of currant are the black ones. Black Currants are a hardy crop, resistant to early and winter frosts and also to drought. What I like especially is that they provide powerful vitamins. For instance, their vitamin C has concentrations four times higher than citrus fruits; their potassium amounts are much higher than other fruits. For these reasons, they are great cold cures. I like their weaving branch structure and beautiful berries."

Brother Alexis ordinarily worked on the abbey farm, in charge of the chickens, ducks and geese, but since it was early spring, he ventured into the pasture near the dairy barn to pick dandelion leaves. He had picked them before for the salads of both monks and students. When Frater Leo heard of picking dandelions, he told his confreres about the value of these so-called weeds.

"While my father detested these healthy plants and used chemicals to kill them in the grain fields, my mother loved them, and I share her appreciation of and sympathy for them. She used them in a brew with orange and lemon slices, raisins, sugar and water; it tasted like a slightly bitter liquor. 'Don't drink too much otherwise you might wet the bed!' she told me.

"She was versatile in using these greens, for in addition to preparing them as salads, she chopped them into my morning porridge where they became emerald specks. Visiting children and adults were puzzled when they were told that there was dandelion in peanut butter sandwiches and muffins.

"When I heard that Brother Alexis was picking them, I wanted to be part of this job and asked Father Martin whether I could help Brother. I received his assent and joined him. The beautiful yellow blossoms were everywhere but the leaves took a while to harvest. 'I think dandelions are really lions and tell us, Hear us roar!' Brother joked. 'Quite different from what you might expect of a being that is regarded as an enemy or as homely.'

"Brother and I went on our hands and knees and waxed eloquent about these wondrous edibles. I always liked their splendid bee-friendly blossoms, and their later puff balls which we children blew at each other. I found attractive their jagged green teeth which gives them their name, the teeth of the lion in French.

"I wanted to know more about them and found that there is scarcely anything positive written. They can be highly valued, for they are full of iron, calcium, vitamins C, A, and folic acid. These golden bouquets benefit the liver and help with the flu. They contain many times more vitamin A than tomato juice. They are great companion plants with the grasses, but we never ate the flowers or roots."

PICKING SASKATOONS

The novices generally did not venture outside of the abbey area; other monks visited nearby farms, pastures and the outskirts of lakes to pick Saskatoon berries. But Father Abbot made an exception and the novices were permitted to join other monks in this task; his rationale was that the need for berries for the students was great and the bushes were now heavy with them.

"When they were in season, I remember our whole family would go to pick them at favorable locations," Frater Tobias reminisced. "We used jam pails as containers, and sometimes the berries were as luscious as grape clusters. We would take lunch along and pick all day. Then in the evening we would clean them of twigs, green berries, stink bugs, lady bird beetles, and discard the worm-eaten ones.

"We used to call them June berries for they started ripening at the end of June. They had a sweet, nutty almond flavor and I was told that our Queen insisted when she visited Canada, we thought for her pre-paid vacation, that she have a few Saskatoon berry pies to take home.

"I was so fascinated with these deep purple berries that I read up about them," Frater Tobias went on. "They are high in fiber and protein, a guard against almost everything including cancer, heart attacks, eye diseases; they also postpone aging. I am told that these berries have more calcium content than red meats, vegetables and cereals. And besides that, they taste so good it would be foolish not to eat them, for they are appetizing right off the bush.

"The name for Saskatoon berries is an adaptation of the Cree word *misaskwatomina* which early white settlers shortened to saskatoon. The Indians used this berry in ceremonies for it had a sacred significance. The places for their spring and summer encampments often favored good picking locations where they collected the berries, dried them and used them in making pemmican. They used the hard, straight-grained wood from Saskatoon bushes for arrow shafts, pipes, basket frames, and the cross pieces of canoes. They also used Saskatoon berries in many medicines: to treat liver trouble and as a laxative, with the inner bark or roots as a remedy for diarrhea. In earlier times, they were also used as a trade item.

"My Mom used them mostly in pies, but also in jams, sauces, and as salad dressing. Some people made wine from them. They can also be canned.

53

"They are often compared to blueberries, but they are quite different and the similarity is mostly because they are of the same color. But there is no comparison. Saskatoon berries sing. They are wild and loud and strong and free.

"People went crazy when they got a call from a friend that they found a patch alongside their farm or along a country road ready for the plucking. They dropped everything and went picking for the time was right.

"Before my time, Indians encamped on the treed northern side of our yard. It was an ideal place in the summer: shaded, next to Saskatoon berry patches, close to the water and buffalos. It is cultivated now, but we found arrowheads and stone hammers in that area and many buffalo heads and bones on the edge of our lake.

"I gathered the bones and sold them to our elevator. They made good glue."

During this monkish picking enterprise, one of them, Father Florian, did not pick many berries but instead walked or drove the van ahead to reconnoiter for more bushes. He returned and pointed to new and flourishing patches. One of these was on the perimeter of a large lake; as he showed it to us, he took off all his clothes and instead of picking berries, waded into the water. Others ventured in up to their knees for the water was warm.

"We were surprised to see this naked monk having a great time in the water," Frater Leo said. "And he took off his clothes so spontaneously, so easily and naturally. I never thought I would see a monk in the nude! And I was a little shocked."

As we picked the berries, mosquitoes buzzed all around. We complained about them, for they were pesky and greedy; we had to briefly interrupt our picking to brush them off for they really liked to get our blood. The bush branches pricked us. As one of us opened the branches of a Saskatoon bush, we saw a skunk's uplifted tail. We closed the bush and hightailed it away quickly.

We ate a prepared lunch and then returned to the abbey with the loot. The Sisters welcomed us and the great amount of berries, even though they had most of the burden to clean and wash them in cold water. On the next day, during the main meal, each of the monks had a bowl of Saskatoon berries, covered with thick, heavy farm cream. A few insects on the bowls' perimeter. No sugar needed. No more complaints about insect bites, gashed skin or skunks. This was a time for celebration! It was worth it.

Later on, fragrant Saskatoon berry pie, a slice, warm out of the oven with some vanilla or maple walnut ice cream. Mmmm. Our Queen was definitely onto something!

HAIRCUTS

While Brother John was the official haircutter, the monastic custom was that all of the novices should learn how to cut hair by practicing on various community members. Brother John diligently tutored each of the novices and hoped there would be some scapegoats, some volunteers, who would trust the novices for a haircut. Frater Callistus was not very digitally skilled and this showed as he attempted to learn barbering skills. His victims came through the clipping ordeal with little crevices in their tonsorial patterns.

"It will grow out in a week or two and you will not know the difference between an amateur and a professional one," he argued. "After all, in previous times, barbers also performed surgery and dentistry!" However, at another event, Frater Callistus' eyesight must have failed him even more as the clipper ventured into the ear of one of his confreres. There was blood and a handkerchief had to mop up and stop further erosion.

Another monk who was very bald did not mind a rough job: "One hair cut only," he joked, since he had so few hair. Some of the monks gave gifts to the novices for their services, such as a candy bar, some suckers or even a cigar, although novices were not permitted to smoke.

Quite often the superiors did not acknowledge past or latent skills of monks, but sometimes the opposite happened. Father Gregory had previously served in a men's clothing store and had attained some skills in measuring garments. This now came in handy as he measured the candidates for their habits. He also knew how to compensate his measurements for changes in weight. Novice candidates who were students in the college came for their measurements during the academic year and those who were from the outside had to make an appointment for this service.

Generally, monks were appointed to positions in parishes, the press, high school and college irrespective of their inclinations or abilities. Appointments were made, instead, according to the needs of the monastic community. Thus, if there was need to fill a position in teaching chemistry or history, as a disciplinarian (a prefect), farm worker, or for advanced studies, any old monk (or young one) was appointed, it seemed. There was scant consultation with the candidate.

PLAYING CARDS

The companion (Socius) for the novices had a passion for playing cards. It's as if the regular monks did not provide sufficient outlet for this need, so he insisted on pursuing this pastime at every opportunity he had with the novices, even twice a day. His beloved game, skat (pronounced skaat), was the one and only game for the Socius. To begin, and that day began on the day of investiture, he gave a brief introduction to skat, a German three-player trick-taking card game. It was created around 1810 in Altenburg (Thuringia), Germany, and for many years was the most popular card game. "It is the best and most interesting game, the king of German card games," the Socius said.

There was one problem with the present setting of the game: only three could play and with the Socius, there were five possible participants. The Socius had an answer to this dilemma: three would participate and two would be observers, would-be participants in waiting. But which three would play initially? The Socius already had a solution. All would pick straws from those he had already concealed in his fingers and hand. The two selecting the longest ones would have the privilege of being the first ones to play with himself.

The Socius then gave a history of the game. "The composer Richard Strauss was a great card player and he even included a round of this game in one of his operas, *Intermezzo*. When Adolf Hitler came to power in 1933, he forbade Jews from playing it and revised the card deck, excluding what he considered cards that were too Jewish. As Germany invaded various European countries, the game spread. Today, although the German influence is mitigated, the game remains, and even has French and Jewish versions.

"The German word, *skat*, not to be confused with the English word, scat, is derived from Latin, *scarto, scartare*, meaning to discard or reject, that is, discard two cards from the deck. I might interject that for some scat/discarding refers to fecal matter. But that is not the case here.

"The game might seem complicated at first, but you will easily catch on. At the beginning of each round or deal, one player becomes the declarer and the other two players become the defending team. The beauty of this game is that one can bid according to his hand and can win even if the hand has the lowest points, a null game, in which the player bids to take no tricks, make no points!

"The goal for each player is to bid a game value as high as their card holding would allow, but never higher than necessary to win."

The Socius introduced German words used in the game such as *Schneider,* announced by declarer after the bidding (declarer has to take 90 or more trick points to win the game), and *Schwarz,* also announced by declarer after the bidding (declarer has to take all tricks to win).

"There is a game variant called *Ramsch* or junk. If all three players pass in the bidding, each player plays for himself and tries to achieve as low a score as possible. The goal of *Ramsch* is to punish players who underbid their hands."

To us it seemed very complicated but the Socius was reassuring. The stakes became higher when he presented a tablet in which he wrote the names of all participants, including himself, and announced that the scores would be recorded and compared with one another. Competition became acute; we tried to avoid having a low recorded score and thereby evade embarrassing comparisons. Skat became the occasion of high tension.

THOSE WHO DO NOT FIT IN

Father Damian was editor of *St. Peter's Messenger* shortly after World War I, during which time he wrote an editorial criticizing Orangeman John Dief-enbaker in his bid for political leadership. Diefenbaker, a lawyer, threatened to take him to court but nothing came of it.

Later, during his retirement, Father Damian reviewed many books for the *Messenger,* often taking comments from the jacket; he translated other books, notably a commentary on the *Rule of St. Benedict.* This commission, it was rumored, occurred because the Abbot could not find meaningful work for him; his war-altering experiences (during which he served as ser-geant) did not permit him to hold positions of long duration in the abbey or college. Because of his affliction, he did not attend daily prayers nor eat at the monastic table but rather at the "second table."

A chain smoker, he could be heard as he shuffled his way loudly through the corridors. He had a great devotion to the Little Flower, St. The-resa of Lisieux and often quoted her: "If you pick up a pin out of love you might save a soul." A frequent visitor to the lunchroom and to the rooms of monks he considered special, he liked to tell jokes but did not enjoy hearing any himself.

There were others in the monastery who did not fit in. One, a priest from another diocese, was called Uncle. He was a simple, congenial guy who picked up religious print material, some soiled, and gave it to visitors to the college and abbey. He was rather deaf and slurped his soup in a most noisy fashion. As I was walking down the monastic corridor, he approached me and wondered whether I would sign his written last will and testament, bequesting his meager savings to the abbey. Innocently, I readily did.

Another, living in the monastic precincts was Father Pepper. At one of the national bishops' meetings that Father Abbot attended, one of the prelates suggested that it was now the monastery's turn to take in this former monk. After all, the prelate noted, the Rule both acknowledges that there will always be roving people, *gyrovagues,* who visit monasteries. The Rule also states that all people should be welcomed as Christ.

How could the Abbot refuse? Here he was, kicked out of his own monastery, exclaustrated as it is called, but now found a room in our monastery. He was a dandy, not permitting the Sisters to launder his shirts; instead, the procurator had to take them to the neighboring town to be dry cleaned. He had studied and spoke several languages and helped tutor a French class, insisting that he be paid, although he was not charged for his room and board.

Some of us liked to make fun of our prime minister, imitating the shaking of his bulbous jowls and head. We had a hard time understanding why Father Pepper took such great exception to our fun-loving antics until we realized that he was a staunch monarchist, an attitude he shared with our prime minister. To make fun of the latter was to make fun of our dear monarch, an association we did not fully grasp.

'HANDLE SMALL THINGS LIKE THE VESSELS OF THE ALTAR'

St. Benedict wrote that monks should take care of everything, even small things, "as vessels of the altar," as sacred things. Be careful in handling equipment, don't break things, don't tear your habit through carelessness, don't overeat. At the monastery, the monks were in charge of their produce to a great extent. They grew vegetables and fruits in their gardens and in the orchard; they produced their own eggs, meat and grain. In the kitchen, the cooks made most of the meals from scratch. There was a lot of work involved in these processes but also a lot of satisfaction and control.

Meals, then, gave great pleasure to all the monks for they were in charge, they were responsible, it was the work of their hands, they were connected, close to nature. In eating, they were savoring the work of their own and their brothers' toil, a way of getting to know one another and a way of giving thanksgiving for the bounty of God.

The head gardener asked Father Martin for help in picking the rather meager growth of green beans. Father Martin singled out Fraters Callistus and Tobias to help gather those greens. Picking was slow and the two of them worked on parallel rows. During this time, Frater Callistus shared one of his travel experiences which involved, he thought, only a few small things.

"A few years ago, I decided to travel to Santo Domingo in the Dominican Republic. I read that it was so central to European exploration, settlement, and trade in the sixteenth century.

"I flew to its capital and booked at the Boutique Hotel Palacio in the Colonial Zone since it was near the center of the city and the Cathedral. It was the first cathedral in the Americas and its cornerstone was laid by Diego Columbus, son of Christopher. Initially slaves could attend the liturgy but were later prohibited because they engaged in frenzied drumming.

"I basked in the sunshine in the nearby Parque Colon with its many pigeons, dogs, stately trees and tourists like myself. There was a painter in the park along with a saxophonist and a man fashioning melon-like hats from palm branches. As I went back to my hotel, I noticed men playing dominoes and chess on the streets. Women did not play, but some watched.

"From Santo Domingo I took a bus to Port-au-Prince, Haiti, for it was on the same island. I noticed increasing poverty as I left the city and approached the next country. In Haiti's capital city I checked in at Coconut Villa Hotel. After I settled in, I took a walk on the immediate street. Three young girls with giddy grins approached me. They knew some rudimentary English and asked me if they could be of service. I looked at them for they were beautiful but poorly dressed. I hesitated for a moment but then said yes. How much, I asked. The first one said $10 American, as did also the second and third. 'Money for family,' one said. I gave them my room number and asked them to meet me there at 10 pm that evening.

"On second thought, I must have been crazy for I was not going to comply with their trade, even for such a small amount. What should I do now? How about giving them a positive experience and so I phoned the desk and asked for two movies, Walt Disney's *Sleeping Beauty,* and *The Hunchback of Notre Dame,* three bags of popcorn, a dozen chocolate bars and eight bottles of Seven up.

"The girls arrived promptly at 10 and nervously shared their names, Marie, Sonia and Immacula. They had garlands in their hair and low-slung blouses. I invited them in and gave each one $10. They were apprehensive but we watched the two movies, ate and drank until 2 am. They were becoming very sleepy and I thanked them for coming.

"On reflecting on this event, I felt good about the experience; I had not abused them. However, in view of the great poverty in the country, I had done very little. I did not relieve their destitution, nor provide them with much hope. However, I remembered Jesus saying that if you give a cup of water, you did it for him. As I thought more on this experience, I felt that God's presence was there in that simple and limited sharing. My boat was so small on that vast ocean, but God was there with us."

BEES

The Rule does not mention the keeping of bees or an apiary but our monastery had one. Brother Dominic was in charge; he procured seminal clusters of bees for 10 hives in the spring, placed them in a first rung of hives facing south and the sun, and near a field of alfalfa.

In the fall, after breakfast, Father Martin came into the novitiate with Brother Dominic who requested two volunteers to help with extracting honey from the bee hives. It was a warm day and ideal for the task. Fraters Tobias and Leo volunteered. Brother gave immediate instructions to these two novices that they had to dress properly for the job.

"Make sure that the bottoms of your pants are secured and your long sleeves are tight at your wrists; use gloves, for bees can easily crawl inside your hands and then they might bite you," Brother Dominic said. "Put on caps and I will give you veils to protect you."

As the novices neared the apiary, Brother Dominic thought he should talk to them again: "Now let me give you a little honey bee knowledge. A hive or colony should have only one queen, a fertile one, who is surrounded by workers who feed and groom her; her only job is to lay eggs, about 1,500 a day, one at a time; she can live three to five years.

"Also in the hive are drones. These are hundreds of males who have no stingers; their task is to mate with the queen and their big eyes help them find her; they die shortly after mating.

"Then there are the workers; these are thousands of infertile females; they live six weeks, clean the hive, feed and nurse the larvae, build and cover the honeycombs (wax cells), ventilate and guard the hive, and collect pollen and nectar.

"These workers make royal jelly, a clear liquid with sugars, proteins and vitamins used to feed the larvae when they are very young. Queens receive it all their lives. Workers make six-sided cells from wax which comes from glands in their abdomen; these cells store honey or eggs. Besides their work in and for the hives, bees cross pollinate many crops including alfalfa, apples, and onions. They are indeed busy bees!

"I need one of you to work with this bee smoker; as you can see, it is a tin container with a spout, lid and bellows. You have to insert this corrugated cardboard into the smoker, light it and keep it burning slowly by squeezing the bellows; this provides a blast of fresh air which feeds the smoldering fuel and produces a cool smoke.

"I use this smoker before and during the opening of a hive; as I open the hive, I watch and listen to the bees and give them a few small puffs which interrupts the colony's defensive response and calms them. These puffs control the bees, move them from getting crushed between these boxes, called supers, stop them from stinging, and prevent them from inciting other bees to join in.

"As you will notice when we take the lid off a hive, the wax cells on both sides of the frames are filled with honey. I want my second novice to help me remove the frames, one at a time. As I remove them, I gently brush the bees from the comb, place them in the cart and take them to the garage."

Brother Dominic had informed and instructed us well. He became excited about the honey extraction process. "Before I or you crank this honey extractor, I have to use a scratcher to remove the wax cappings. These frames have honey on both sides, so each side needs to be uncapped.

"Help me place four uncapped frames into the metal mesh baskets in the extractor. Now you can use the handle to crank it. The honey is forced out of the comb and drips down the inside of the extractor. Once the spinning stops, we take the frames out and flip them so that honey is removed from the other side.

"When honey starts filling up the bottom of the extractor, I will open the valve and let honey flow into the waiting bucket. Then I filter the honey through a strainer. There is a lot of wax from the cappings which can be used for making lotions and furniture polish.

"This is the honey that monks and students use at table; it is also used for baking. I don't heat it for that destroys its healthy ingredients," Brother concluded.

Now Fraters Tobias and Leo found new meaning to the honey on their table next morning.

The Divine Office

MATINS

IN THEIR EVENING PRAYERS, we monks anticipated the longer part of the Divine Office, the midnight/morning prayer, Matins. Depending on the feast and/or season of the year, it was longer or shorter. When it was longer, that is, three nocturnes or phases, we called it a three ringer.

After the opening prayer, a psalm of invitation followed, to be recited slowly, according to the rubrics (directives), in consideration for late-arriving monks. Then there were two sets of psalms, followed by readings from the *Old* or *New Testament* or from the Church Fathers. Each reading was followed by a response.

One monk was the leader of these prayers for a week; he was aptly called a hebdomadarian, from Latin, *hebdomada*, week.

LAUDS

After awakening and rushing into church, we prayed a sunrise prayer, Lauds, meaning praise. We praised God for the new light, Christ, and for Jesus rising from the dead. Indeed, we monks were rising from the dead, or more or less.

"God is the light, the source, and shines in each person," Father Martin commented. "Everyone embodies that light, shares in it and can become the prism to refract that light in myriad ways. Just as monks celebrate evening prayer with the sun setting in the west, they celebrate morning prayer with the sun rising in the east, the dawn of God's creation."

During Lauds, the prayer leader chanted the daily martyrology, a listing of the lives of saints which included Benedictines. This chant proved challenging for three reasons: one, the chanter had to overcome his sleepiness; two, there were tongue twisters in the Latin text; three, the narration for each saint ended with a quint, the dropping of five notes in the chant, hard for some at any time of the day but especially this early in the morning.

BENEDICTUS

Included in these prayers was the *Benedictus* from the *Gospel of Luke;* it is one of the three canticles in the opening chapters of Luke's Gospel, the other two being the *Magnificat* and *Nunc Dimittis.* The *Benedictus* was the song of thanksgiving uttered by Zechariah on the occasion of the circumcision of his son, John the Baptist.

This canticle receives its name from its first words in Latin, *Benedictus Dominus Deus Israel,* Blessed be the Lord God of Israel. Christ comes as the rising sun, for monks now pray while standing. It is also used at funerals, at the moment of interment, as words of thanksgiving for redemption, or as an expression of Christian hope at the end of life.

Then we pray the *Pater Noster,* the Our Father; it holds a special place toward the end of Lauds, as it does in Vespers. All monks are obliged to live in its spirit of forgiveness. A great context for the celebration of Mass which follows.

The main Mass of the day is called the conventual Mass; all monks attend, but only the celebrant partakes of the consecrated bread and wine. After the conclusion of this Mass, individual priests celebrate their Masses at private altars. The Brothers serve at these Masses, but one of the novices, each for a week at a time, serves the Abbot's Mass at the main altar.

It was my turn to serve at the beginning of this specific week and I helped the Abbot put on his vestments. He noticed that the amice, a cloth to cover his neck and shoulders, was not immediately available on the proper hanger.

"You should put the amice on top so that it is close at hand," the Abbot commanded me.

Father Abbot did not realize that it was the previous novice who had tucked the amice under the alb, and that I was not responsible for misplacing it. But, noting the Abbot's misjudgment and his inappropriate correction, I decided to absorb the remark as part of learning to be humble. I heard later from the Rule that the abbot should temper his remarks and actions so that he does not break the bruised reed. I had to admit that in some way he did just that. I don't know how this experience fits into St. Benedict's stages of humility, but it somehow fits in for me, I thought.

Altogether there were eight daily prayer services. I already considered the first one, Lauds; after that, shorter prayers, the "first hour" called Prime, recalled the 6 am beginning of the day in times past; then Terce, the third hour; Sext, the sixth hour, recited just before noon; and None, the ninth hour, or 3 pm, recited right after the noon meal.

VESPERS

The monks' evening prayer is called Vespers, celebrated at 5:30 and comprising mostly of recited or chanted psalms. Concluding Vespers is Mary's hymn, *Magnificat*. "It is recorded only in Luke's infancy narrative," Father Martin said, "one of three hymns, distilled from a collection of early Jewish-Christian canticles; it complements the promise-fulfillment theme of Luke's infancy narrative. In form and content, these canticles are patterned on the 'hymns of praise' in Israel's psalter. In structure, these songs reflect the compositions of pre-Christian contemporary Jewish hymnology.

"I regard the *Magnificat* as the best canticle because its words sum up all Christianity and monasticism," Father Martin commented. "In English, this song begins with 'My soul proclaims the greatness of the Lord.' It is perhaps the earliest of Marian hymns. Mary proclaims these words when she visits her cousin Elizabeth who is pregnant with John the Baptist and who praises Mary for her faith; Mary responds with what we now know as the *Magnificat*.

"I like the contrasts in this song of reversals: the proud will be brought low, the humble will be lifted up, and the rich will go empty.

"For me, Mary symbolizes both ancient Israel and the Lucan faith-community. She responds so well to God's physical presence and his growth within her, feeding on her and on all of creation.

"In a style like *Hebrew Testament* poetry and song, Mary praises the Lord: she rejoices that she has the privilege of giving birth to the promised Messiah. She glorifies God for his power, holiness, and mercy. She exalts God because he has been faithful to his promise made to Abraham.

"The *Magnificat* reaches out both to the past and to the future; it is retrospective and prophetic at the same time. Her song announces not only the birth of Christ, but also the birth of a new liberated people whose life will be centered on the spirit of life.

"Besides the *Benedictus* and *Magnificat* there is a third song in Luke's Gospel, Simeon's *Nunc Dimittis*. It is fittingly used during evening prayers. Simeon, a devout Jew, had been promised by the Holy Spirit that he would not die until he had seen the Messiah.

"When Mary and Joseph brought Jesus to the temple in Jerusalem for the purification rite, Simeon took the baby into his arms, blessed God and uttered these words: 'Now, Master, you can let your servant go in peace *[Nunc Dimittis]*, just as you promised; because my eyes have seen the salvation which you have prepared for all the nations to see, a light to enlighten the pagans and the glory of your people Israel.'"

Then, Father Martin gave an additional elaboration: "Whenever God chooses to establish his dwelling-place in a human heart, he stamps it with two of his own characteristic features, that is, with the attitudes of thanksgiving and with sharing. The first feature–thanksgiving–refers to God in praise for his gift; the second feature helps us to reach out and share this gift with other human beings."

The chants or recitations occurred in the chapel with a dialogue of one side of the choir succeeded by the other side, with antiphons/short phrases or sentence sung or recited.

We novices took some time to get used to the Divine Office, maybe we never got used to it. St. Benedict called it the work of God, *Opus Dei,* in Latin. There was a great physicality to it, for everyone, well almost everyone, the novices for sure, heeded the early bell. It seemed that nobody ever had enough sleep, never long enough sleep, always sleep deprived. We young-uns needed more than seven hours a night. We felt that a snooze sometime during the day would fit the bill, but we were forbidden to do so unless we were ill. Some of us put our heads down on our desks and slept for a few minutes. Sleeping in this unnatural position was not comfortable, but there was no delay in falling fast sleep even amid noises.

At this early hour of the morning, most monks forced themselves to get up, go to the bathroom, shave if they had to, wash, put on their habits and goad themselves to the chapel, very deliberately; they greeted no one that early in the morning. There was real devotion here, spending a lot of time first thing in the morning, a stark focus on God.

In chapel, I perused again–for I had studied it the day before or everyday–the specific feast day or the seasons of the church year, all specified in a small yearly booklet called the *Ordo*. In my pew or choir stall, I opened the monastic prayer book, the breviary, to the right places; put ribbons where both the common or everyday texts, and the proper texts, those pertaining to the specific day, were found. But there was an appeal to this ritual as it became habitual and easier; I was often mesmerized by the recitations and the chants, even entranced. At other times, the Office was just too long, too repetitious, too demanding.

Then there was singing both in the Office and during the celebration of Mass. The singing was, apart from some stellar voices, quite average, but sometimes it came together to make a moving experience, showing that despite differences, or because of them, monks could get together, especially for this work of God. There were annoyances such as the monks who could not get the pitch right, as in chanting the martyrology. Or the eccentric monk who insisted on chanting faster or slower than the others. Or sitting and standing beside a monk who hardly ever washed. All this weird behavior merged with singing and prayer. Yes, this was, ideally for monks, the work of God, their primary vocation.

In fact, Benedict stated that nothing was to be preferred to this action. Everything else could be interrupted: caring for the sick, teaching, parish work, manual labor on the farm and garden. This round of prayer, the Office, could/should become unceasing, without sloth or haste throughout the day, the week, month, year, and, for the monks, centuries, for Benedict wrote the Rule in 529 AD.

After night prayers, there was the great silence beginning after Matins in the evening until after breakfast, except in emergencies. Monks on a journey or with a ministry outside the monastery tried to keep these hours, praying privately, but with the intention of participating in the community's prayers.

There were always monks who came late for prayer, novices not too often. There was a provision for tardiness: if one arrived after the first psalm, one had to kneel between the choirs for the space of an Our Father and Hail Mary and then bow to both sides before taking his place. However, while kneeling one monk fell asleep. The Abbot noticed this and asked a novice to tap him on the shoulder to wake up and take his place in his choir stall.

We were told the following story from another much larger monastery. It was warm both outside and inside the church while the monks were praying, so the doors were open. A dog wandered into the worship area, moved between the choirs, seemed to be a monk for it appeared to bow to both sides and sat down in the middle, enjoying the Divine Office.

The dog stayed a while and the Abbot noticed it. He motioned to a novice and whispered to him, "Kick the mutt out of here." The novice, adhering to strict obedience, went up to the dog and gave it a swift boot which caused much yelping but to the great amusement of all of the monks, except the Abbot.

While standing in the choir stalls, monks could rest their weary bones, at least their posteriors, on a protrusion on the stall seat, rightly called a *misericords*, a merciful support. But there were monks who were half asleep or fully asleep during prayers and readings.

One monk, we were told, collapsed in his stall, seemingly from a faint. His prayer stall was quite far away from the aisle and well into the choir; this posed a challenge to extricate him; consequently, fellow monks elevated him and thus carried him out of the church, in a quasi-ceremonial procession. Prayers were interrupted. Some monks were amazed; others were disturbed, others snickered. After this event, the carriers put him down in the sacristy, a room for vestments and sacred vessels; he awoke, opened his eyes and wondered what all the fuss was about. He had not fainted but had fallen fast asleep!

While there were other levities during these solemn prayers, and events sometimes provoked giggles because it was supposed to be so solemn, the ceremonials also engendered mystical experiences. For these monks, while praying the liturgy, it seemed as if the liturgy itself was praying through them, a blessed experience. They felt they were experiencing realities beyond themselves. Of course, a more sanguine interpretation was that although one was enraptured, as one might be in a musical production or a movie, it was still a down-to-earth experience. And there might be the interpretation that one was merely half-conscious or even somewhat delirious.

Father Martin elaborated on the importance of the Divine Office. He quoted from the *Acts of the Apostles*, the account where Peter and John went up to the temple at the ninth hour to pray. He intimated that the psalms and canticles that we recited and sang in this Office were dictated by the Holy Ghost himself so that we might praise and glorify God. Certainly, this praise, then, would be very acceptable to God, for it was using his very words to praise himself! To justify such logic, the novice master paraphrased Psalm 51, that the sacrifice of praise shall glorify God.

Such singing of psalms and hymns is also the occupation of the angels, specifying the *Prophet Isaiah* and the *Apocalypse,* as angels surround the throne of God adoring, praising and glorifying him. In this Office, then, we are joining the family of angels in their harmonies (and disharmonies?) in heaven.

The psalms and hymns also mirror every circumstance of life and the stages of the spiritual life. The unlettered in the early church memorized and used them, as we were prone to do.

When he delved into the psalms, Father Martin said that they were really Christian prayer; they form the longest part of the Divine Office. "Many know the psalms, *De Profundis* and *Miserere Mei Deus,* but have little knowledge of the entire 150 of them. The *De Profundis* is a penitential psalm, a song of sorrow for misdeeds, a prayer for courage, a prayer for the dead.

The other psalm, the *Miserere,* is based on an incident in the *Second Book of Samuel* where King David meets the prophet Nathan who rebukes him for his two sins: adultery with Bathsheba and the killing of her husband, Uriah. David sings God's praises as he asks for forgiveness. So, this confession is regarded as a model of repentance, for those who sin and pray to God will be forgiven. The *Miserere* is a guide for morally weak human beings on how to ask forgiveness and return to God's grace. It can be recited in acute distress as both Thomas More and Lady Jane Grey prayed it before their executions.

"In *the Miserere,* God desires a broken and contrite heart more than he does sacrificial offerings," Father Martin said. "However, our dark spirit should reflect our contrition but not degenerate into depression. Some time should be given to repentance but the rest of the day you should be joyful.

"The *Miserere* has a prominent place in many Roman Catholic celebrations such as the Divine Office, funeral celebrations which call for divine mercy for the deceased. Part of the *Miserere* forms the invocation and chant in the Greek, *Kyrie eleison,* Lord have mercy, which begins the Mass. Also, while we process at noon from the refectory, we recite it.

"In this psalm, the phrase, *Asperges me,* wash me, is used as the liturgical minister sprinkles holy water on the faithful during the entrance ritual of the Mass, symbolizing the cleansing of the people."

"I like Psalm 8 especially," Frater Tobias mused, "because it is short, but notably for its sweeping spirit recognizing God's grandeur. It has a great lilting sound in Latin."

Father Martin noted that the psalms have a universal application in the life of church members. Here he quoted St. John Chrysostom: "When the faithful have a vigil at the Church, David [the reputed psalm composer] is at the beginning, in the middle and at the end. If at dawn they wish to sing hymns, it is again David who begins, continues and concludes. In funeral processions and at funeral services, it is David who is first and last. David and his psalms are never lost or forgotten."

"The psalms are the epitome of *Hebrew Testament* revelation," Father Martin stated. "Their character is that they are either a song of praise or a lamentation or a combination of the two. They recall vividly the theme of the redemption of Israel and the conquest of Israel's enemies. In recounting the latter, they are sometimes filled with emotions of violence and vindictiveness, pleading for the destruction of Israel's enemies; this can stir feelings of repugnance in us. One of my confreres noted that when things don't go right, or when he has a grievance against a fellow monk, he takes glee in these psalms for they express his very sentiments.

"Today the psalms reveal our faith in God's completion of and his fidelity to his promises through Jesus Christ. We also want to see and possess the promised land but we have a new meaning to the holy war. It is not a matter of vindictiveness, although we lament the attacks of our opponents. We now must love our enemies and do good to those who persecute us. We also oppose the false gods who will lead us astray. With the Israel of old, together with the psalmist, we want to see God glorified, a new heaven and a new earth and hope to arrive in the promised land."

Part of our spiritual exercises was not only to pray the psalms but also to study them. The Socius was commissioned to do this. All of us knew that he was extremely busy with teaching and working in the gardens, but we expected that he would work with us in understanding the psalms in their Hebrew context, or maybe even translate them from the Latin texts or discuss their relevance. But no, he came in every week, sat down at the desk and asked us to copy in long hand the commentary he proceeded to give us. He did not meet our expectations and we were quite miffed that we had to undergo a grade school process of slavishly writing down his words. However, we did not complain about the process; it was part of our general submission. None of us cherished or reread these scribblings.

The *Tyrocinium*

Father Martin used a late nineteenth-century book, the *Tyrocinium,* as a guide for us to live the religious life; it gave instructions on how to use the proper means to avoid sin and practice virtue. Written by a Benedictine, the *Tyrocinium* is based on the *Rule of St. Benedict.* Each novice received a copy and we followed the sections the novice master pointed to.

There was a section on authority. Although God himself is the real teacher, his representative on earth, the abbot, takes his place and is to be obeyed. The Holy Ghost uses the abbot as his interpreter and organ, to work now in the church militant to lead to the heavenly church triumphant. The abbot alone in the monastery has a private pipeline to the Holy Spirit. When he speaks, he also has centuries of law on his side. The obedience he demands is difficult for there are many obstacles to compliance, such as pride, love of the world, sloth, an aversion to labor, fear of difficulties, neglect of earnest mortification (interior and exterior), ingratitude for graces and favors, reliance on one's own strength and want of confidence in God.

Novices were to have little or no interaction with fellow monks; they were to live in relative isolation, associating only with one another, with the novice master, their confessor, and the abbot. Was that because they might be scandalized by the activities of other monks, or would the novices scandalize the fervent ones?

There are many things a novice should avoid, the *Tyrocinium* exhorted, such as unnecessary contacts with the world and mundane-minded persons; useless and secular conversations; frivolity and petulant forwardness; idle and unnecessary roaming outside the novitiate; excess in eating and drinking, private and sensual friendships and familiarities. On the other hand, the novice should endeavor to keep himself well disposed toward God, to his neighbor and to himself.

Father Martin put a lot of focus on the importance of attaining merit. There were two sources of merit, he thought. One source was procured by acting according to the virtue of religion. As far as we could tell, this virtue followed from our baptism as Christians. We act according to that grace and we pile up merit by doing so. However, we could multiply that merit by taking vows, the second source of merit. When we obey, we double the merit, increase our bank account of grace. So, it made sense to take vows because of that accumulation of cash in the form of grace. This seemed to make sense although we had an inkling that Martin Luther might have had some objections to this and so we were a little confused.

GENERAL CONFESSION

We went to confession each week and generally to Father Martin. But he was away this particular week, so we went to Father Prior. He was a short, elderly monk with a long, white pointed beard and dark-rimmed granny glasses. A founder of this monastery and a long-time editor of the German weekly, *St. Peter's Bote*. I knelt before his desk, confessed my faults and sins and while he gave me an admonition, my eyes wandered over his dust-laden desk and upon a yard-long ruler and a printer's scissors. After my confession, he told me he wanted to show me some things. He took me to his waste barrel, a large cardboard one in which he pointed out a blood-laden mass which he had spit out, and a tuft of hair under his pillow, a remnant of the founder of the original priory; he had passed away some 60 years ago. Then, forgetful of his previous showing, he again took me to the waste barrel to show me the mass. I felt queasy, bade him farewell and, next week, eagerly welcomed my regular confessor.

In addition to making this weekly confession to one's spiritual guide, God's representative, Father Martin said that one should begin the novitiate by making a general confession. To do so was commendable, the *Tyrocinium* recommended, as a means of the re-formation, re-direction, of the whole man and as a means of beginning with a purity of conscience.

In a general confession, we examine all the sins committed after baptism. Obviously, one had to re-confess all mortal sins, even though they were confessed before. The novice master enumerated the usefulness and merit of such an enterprise: one acquires humility, an increase of grace, a complete remission of temporal punishments, a greater purity of soul and a more perfect knowledge and hatred of self.

This general process of reviewing one's past life could engender some negativity, however, and therefore some caution was necessary for one could become quite scrupulous in this process. While one should avoid a lax conscience, one should strive to acquire a tender one, but not to the extent of losing a sense of peace. Novices needed the help of one's confessor to achieve this delicate balance.

As usual, Father Martin did not allot any time for discussion about these points, but during recreation, novices showed their concern about the merit of self- hatred. For those of us who were trying to achieve a direction for ourselves and had encouragement from our parents, we thought a direction other than hatred of self might be possible and even necessary, that is, an affirmation of what we had already achieved and who we already were. Some of us had a little knowledge about the Greek stoics who tried to achieve an equilibrium in their lives by not getting their gizzards either too hot or too cold. This seemed to be a wholesome direction to follow.

Father Martin talked about avoiding distractions. He noted the necessity to use the proper means to avoid them in the novitiate and the benefits that would thereby accrue: peace and tranquility of mind as one excludes inordinate passions and attachments; this is often obtained by a persevering and generous practice of mortification, abnegation of self-love and by a renunciation of the world; a careful and rigid custody of the senses, especially of the eyes (more on this later); practicing recollection joined with spiritual reading so that the mind may be filled with holy thoughts and thereby elicit pious aspirations; elevating the mind to God; with a humble, ardent and constant prayer, saying to Jesus, Lord, teach us how to pray.

The master said he would elaborate on some of these points later on. As we left class we had some ideas in mind: one was that some of the monks that we saw did not seem to exhibit these virtuous characteristics; also, some of these points might be regarded as quite negative, although most of us were not about to make any criticisms.

STAGES OF PURGATION, ILLUMINATION AND UNION

In another talk, Father Martin again followed the *Tyrocinium*: Ascetic writers are wont to distinguish three stages or divisions on the way to perfection, namely, purgation, illumination and union. Pursuing these stages is like becoming virtuous on various levels, like plants and animals that have their beginnings, their growth, and their final perfection.

Novices are at the beginning stage of spiritual growth; they are like plants, just germinating. Only later might they blossom and then mature. At this stage, which spiritual writers call the period of purgation, serious novices have to undergo a mortification of the senses. To those who enter this stage of perfection the Holy Ghost addresses these words of Psalm 36: Decline from evil. These beginners are directed to remove everything that may be an obstacle to an ardent and enduring love of God.

"We have already spoken about the necessity for a general confession," Father Martin began. "We shall examine in turn each one of the senses that can be an obstacle to the process of purification and see how each one can be purged. We call this initial stage the mortification of the senses and we begin with that of sight. The *Book of Ecclesiasticus* says, 'Is anything in creation greedier than the eye? That is why it waters on every occasion.'

"Sight can be considered one of the most dangerous of the senses because it can create more vivid pictures than any other organ. Unguarded glances can become mired in the soul and continue to inflict wounds for many years. For St. Benedict, idle thoughts, distractions, rash judgments and evil desires are the result of an unguarded eye. So, one should never look upon the private parts of one's body without necessity. Gaze not on a person or attire of the opposite sex. Do not stare upon, fondle or caress children. Practice guarding your eyes, *custos occulorum*. When you see the beauties of nature, think of the eternal beauty of their Creator.

"Next, we consider mortification of the sense of hearing. Such a purging is necessary in order to prevent the inclusion of distracting thoughts which might disturb us in our prayers, might arouse our passions. As St. Benedict writes, 'No one should presume to relate to anyone else what he saw or heard outside the monastery, because that causes the greatest harm.' If one hears dirty jokes, one should not continue to listen to them, but change the conversation or command the perpetrator to cease at once.

"Do not listen to murmurers. Do not be anxious to hear gossip, rumors or news of the world which might destroy the spirit of recollection. Learn to love positive stories and to accept and even embrace corrections instead of reacting with impatience and disdain.

"Mortification of the sense of taste. Pampering the sense of taste results in promoting the indulgence of the flesh against that of the spirit. *Plenus venter non studet libenter,* a well-filled stomach does not study well.

In tasting food and drink we should observe moderation in quantity and be indifferent as to its quality, even abstaining from good things. Partake of delicacies abstemiously if at all. In practice, do not be greedy in eating, for the temperate person will live a long life. Do not complain about your food. Do not eat between meals without necessity and don't keep food close at hand. Observe good manners and pay attention to the table reading.

"Mortification of the sense of smell. Again, we move forward largely by way of negation. We sin through the sense of smell by inhaling agreeable odors for mere gratification. We mortify this sense by denying ourselves the pleasure of smelling pleasant odors without cause and even by inhaling disagreeable ones. Use of perfumes or aromatics is not permitted for monks. If you must use tobacco or snuff, do so with moderation. If your job includes smelling foul air, don't complain.

"Mortification of the sense of touch. Again, some negativity: Don't touch the private parts of your body without necessity. Don't indulge in touching in a prolonged manner any person of the opposite sex. Don't stroke animals such as cats or dogs."

"Was Father Martin really serious about this last command?" Frater Tobias wondered. "I noticed that he smirked a little at the end. He must have petted animals on his mixed farm; I certainly petted the dogs and puppies, cats and kittens, horses and cows on our farm. That form of affection seemed appropriate then and I didn't see myself changing now."

"A lot of evil comes from the tongue," Father Martin continued, "so the wise person should carefully consider when to speak and when to be silent, according to St. Bonaventure. He should weigh every word twice, avoiding lies and boasting. According to the *Book of Proverbs*, 'My mouth proclaims the truth, wickedness is hateful to my lips.'

"Protect the good name of others especially those absent. As we saw in the Rule, we should avoid all bombast and noise, but observe silence. Avoid sins against fraternal charity. Manifest the same gentleness toward all, be they great or small, superior or inferior, learned or unlearned. Don't indicate inordinate passion in responding. Don't answer questions before they are asked, for according to Proverbs, 'He that answers before he hears, shows himself to be a fool and worthy of confusion.'

"Mortification of the intellect. Regulate the inner man and then make the outer follow the inner. The premise is that the will is blind and follows the bidding of the intellect. So, get the intellect in order. We should not seek the things that are too high for us and above our abilities. Don't be too curious, observing the doings of our confreres and one's superior with a spirit of unfriendly criticism which may engender rash judgments. We are not appointed judges over our fellowmen.

"Mortify our judgments and interpret the words and actions of others in a spirit of charity. Those who are proud and stubborn are pests in a community; their spirit can lead to factions and strife. Forget things of the past, home, parents, friends. Don't worry about what may be in store for you or concern yourself inordinately about others; pray for them; let the dead bury their dead.

"It is hard to empty oneself of social routines and conventions for these thoughts and desires will surface; instead, be attentive to God," Father Martin advised. "Former selves and desires lurk in the background, always waiting to break through a new monastic identity."

The novices had misgivings about some of these directives. Frater Tobias both eagerly awaited letters from home and also had concerns about family members. These letters transported him to a previous life and often related to inconsequential matters. These matters still had a pull, but were becoming tenuous for they were sometimes petulant, trivial, and banal. They brought up haunting memories which he now regarded as baggage. Even without these reminders, he found it hard to suppress non-spiritual desires and easily remembered the little gratifications of going downtown with a friend and buying candy bars. Although he did not receive any gifts, the letters still reminded him of a past life

"Inordinate love of self leads to self-will," Father Martin said. "So, do all things promptly and cheerfully. Embrace the common exercises of the community. Don't murmur. Do disagreeable things with alacrity. Ask permission of major things. Observe the order of the day and other regulations.

"Always preserve a modest posture of the body when standing, sitting, or, when lying in bed, prefer a hard one. Bear patiently hardships such as cold, heat or sickness."

"I noticed that there were a lot of do's and don'ts," Frater Leo remarked during recreation. "I don't take well to commands because I have an independent spirit."

And then Father Martin gave some general counsel: "Cultivate a true and tender conscience which is not scrupulous or lax. Discipline, enforced over a period of time, might lead to a dependence on external regulations, to lost autonomy, an inability to use the freedom one has to be creative. If you really want to walk on the way of perfection, you should bring the exterior person into harmony with the interior one. That presumes that the interior is on the way of perfection.

"According to St. Benedict, virtues arise from a practical remembrance of the presence of God; this is the foundation for exterior and interior humility and peace. You will then become a light of/to the world and your light will shine before all so that they may see your good works and glorify your Father in heaven. This is the way toward a conversion of morals that Benedict writes about.

"This is good in theory but what about monastic practice? Yes, the practice of humility and being of a good nature takes practice," Father Martin confessed. "We have to be humble enough not to take things too personally. Then, big things, or even little things, such as the singing out of tune, a careless gesture, a gruff answer can be taken with a good nature and not lead to misinterpretation, ill-will or cliquish arguments and disputes. Then these will not become stumbling blocks to a harmonious life in the monastic vocation."

Father Martin did not spend any time on the other ascending ways toward perfection, that of the illuminative and unitive, but he referred to Reginald Garrigou-Lagrange's work on this topic, a volume in the novitiate library.

FOUR LAST THINGS

During the time of Advent, that is, the four Sundays/weeks before Christmas, Father Martin suggested we follow a liturgical tradition and meditate on the Four Last Things, that is, death, judgment, heaven, and hell, a person's four last stages in life and the afterlife. "This tradition is embedded in the Benedictine way of life and is a type of meditation which follows the injunction, Remember your last end and you shall never sin. While the focus most of the time is on an individual's own life, we can also think of the last things as an event at the end of time."

Death

St. Benedict is often regarded as the patron of a happy death. The outer edge of the Benedictine medal contains the words (in Latin), "May we at our death be fortified by his presence." Supported by his fellow monks, Benedict died standing, with arms raised to heaven.

In his Rule, St. Benedict does not speculate about what happens to the body and soul at death, nor does he consider its inevitable connection with original sin. His advice to his monks is more day-to-day, practical. With the Lord he writes, "I do not wish the death of the sinner, but that he turn back to me and live."

For St. Benedict, as for St. Jerome, thoughts about death should be omnipresent. In his chapter, The Tools for Good Works, he notes that "Day by day remind yourself that you are going to die." In the chapter on Restraint of Speech, he quotes *Proverbs*, "The tongue holds the key to life and death." Speaking and teaching are the master's task; the disciple is to be silent and listen. Speaking too much, or saying the wrong things, can lead to death; listening, or holding one's tongue, can lead to life.

Writing about the desires of the body, St. Benedict reminds monks that "God is always with us. . . We must then be on guard against any base desire, because death is stationed near the gateway of pleasure."

In the fourth step of humility, he writes that "obedience under difficult, unfavorable, or even unjust conditions, [the monk] embraces suffering and endures it without weakening or seeking escape." Being brave, enduring suffering even contradiction for the Lord's sake is like death.

St. Benedict extends the meaning of death in this life to the spiritual realm. In some way, the soul dies if the monks are dishonest in dealing with others; there should be no avarice, but monks should provide goods and services to outsiders for a little lower price than usual.

Judgment

At death each Christian is judged according to his conduct in life, but he is also judged at the end of time when all people will rise again. God's plan for the world will then be revealed with the demonstration of his mercy and justice.

In the Rule, the abbot is often the focus for words on judgment. The abbot's teaching, both in words and action, becomes the model for Christian life. If he is understanding and merciful, he will merit mercy himself.

There is a lot of wise advice in the chapter on The Tools for Good Works which pertain to all the monks including the abbot: "And finally, never lose hope in God's mercy. These, then, are the tools of the spiritual craft. When we have used them without ceasing day and night and have returned them on judgment day, our wages will be the reward the Lord has promised: 'What the eye has not seen nor the ear heard, God has prepared for those who love him.'"

Heaven

In his lengthy consideration of humility, Benedict considers life in this world as an ascending ladder through humility to life everlasting. We descend by exaltation and ascend by humility. Even now the monk is in God's sight. Heaven is the Christian's homeland.

Hell

St. Benedict writes about the pains of hell, the fear of hellfire and its dread. It is self-will and an evil zeal which leads to hell. But he also writes about a transformation of the motives from the fear of hell to the love of Christ. For this purpose, he has set up a school for the Lord's service.

In our monastery, the first of these four things, death, was before our eyes through the death of fellow monk, Father Chrysostom. For a brief time, he had been editor of the monastic paper, then returned to the monastery from parish work since he found it increasingly difficult to walk, feed himself or say Mass. On occasion, one of us was asked to serve his Mass. It was a bit tricky for he had a long, pointy white beard which tended to move upward with the static electricity engendered during his vesting. So, he had to pat his beard down periodically.

He was confined to a monastic room and continued to pray his breviary (the clerical/monastic prayer book). Brother Francis brought him his meals from the kitchen. He often grumbled about them, complaining that the toast was too dark or too light, the egg hard or too soft, the soup too bland or too spicy. On one occasion, to Brother Francis' surprise, he was most agreeable about his meal. Brother then suggested he pen a note to the Sisters in the kitchen and thank them for his meals. "I couldn't do that," he retorted. "I don't want to get too friendly with the Sisters!"

We were alerted that Father Chrysostom was dying and some of his fellow monks gathered in his room while others milled through his open door into the corridor for the sacrament of Extreme Unction; it was the last anointing customarily given when a Catholic was near death.

We had heard of a contemporary interpretation of this sacrament. It involved an earlier and less dire anointing of the sick especially when the subject was elderly, conscious and responsive. In his preamble to the action and interpretation of the sacrament, Father Abbot told us that Father Chrysostom had already prepared himself with a general confession of his sins. "This sacrament of anointing," he stated, "has a threefold purpose: to remit all sins, to strengthen the soul for imminent death or, possibly, to restore health."

After this instruction, Father Abbot proceeded to anoint each of Father Chrysostom's bodily organs with the words: "Through this holy unction, and his own tender mercy, may the Lord pardon you whatever sins or faults you have committed by sight (by hearing, smell, taste, touch, walking, and carnal delectation)." We novices learned later that in certain countries the loins were also anointed, but of course, everywhere forbidden in the case of women. This latter information stirred our imagination as to how and intimate such an anointing might be.

TORPOR

Father Martin sensed Frater Callistus' frustration and in his lecture tried to allay its strength. He gave a talk on *acedia*, calling it a noonday devil, a mental and spiritual torpor or apathy.

"No matter what station in life, things can become humdrum and routine. They can lose their vitality and their meaning. We envision a time when this dark force within us looks elsewhere as we feel like dry bread, as we think we are wasting our time. We become distracted during spiritual reading; we dream of a better place, a better time. Nothing is really going on in our lives. Even after adequate sleep, we wake up parched; we have grumpy mornings. Some call this the dark night of the soul. But this darkness, this sadness is not necessarily evil.

"Let it wrap itself around you and penetrate your insides. Wallow in it, let it wind its way insidiously through and around you."

Frater Callistus could easily associate himself with these sentiments.

"While the isolation in the novitiate can cause a lot of psychological stress," Father Martin continued, "it can also lead to something wholesome, a deeper or wider level of consciousness, an interior compensation or reward from the deprivation of the senses. Pray to Archangel Michael to guide you and give you strength during this darkness.

"Advisors about this condition of *acedia* say we should try meditation, deep breathing, fresh air and good nutrition. *Acedia* can be an instrument for good, for growth, however. Don't rely on excessive sleep and wine and food for they merely provide fleeting happiness.

"But what if one doesn't want to be cheered up, to strive to be happy? This can be a time to tap into our creativity and imagination. Good examples are Theresa of Avila and John of the Cross. Learn from the experience of darkness. Use it to connect with your own humanity and with others. A dark night of the soul can heal.

"One can manage it, one can come out transformed. Cracks in one's life can reveal weakness, but cracks can also let the light in. Maybe this is a form of death, an integral part of life which can lead to a termination of the old, to new life and completeness.

"Simply surrender to this uncanny feeling, bask in solitude, talk to your spiritual advisor. You might not emerge a hero in what you might perceive as a grand battle but you will be transformed. You don't have to do something!"

"Most of Father Martin's advice went beyond my understanding," Frater Callistus said. "So, I acknowledged that this was my season of loss, darkness and cold and I hoped for some possession, some light, some cozy feeling. What did I do? I went into the cold outside, stomped in the snow, shivered in the cold. Now I am ready for something new I shouted.

"I began to appreciate these long, dark days of winter. Sometimes I felt dopey and complacent and thought of going into hibernation. But then the cold and snow invigorated me as it tingled my skin, even under my long johns and thick parka. I began to feel alive.

"From these experiences I regarded winter as a special time of the year, quite different from the other seasons. It cleared my head. I began to think more deeply because I had to slow down. I could not dash outside but had to put clothes and boots on and take them off again. I felt great about conquering the elements but also submitting to them. What a delight to read a book, clean out my desk when it's snowing outside.

"I realized that winter won't last forever. Warm days will arrive, deeply appreciated because of the contrast with winter, a time to smile, a time of blossoming. I opened the windows and doors at the first smell of spring. Winter had become a honeymoon phase.

"Wait, I have to end these romantic feelings about winter and the advent of spring, for we are inside and we have to get back to the spiritual battles we were considering."

In his next session, Father Martin referred to a poem by the sixteenth-century Spanish mystic and poet, St. John of the Cross. "We have the dark night of the soul because darkness represents the fact that the destination, God, is unknowable. Even the path to God is unknowable. But the dark night is a purging process for the body and the mind; during this process, natural cares are stilled. First, the sensory parts are purged; one might not feel like eating or drinking anymore; there is no savor to anything."

"I remember the stoics in my introductory course in philosophy," Frater Tobias mused. "This seems much like them although they pursued temperance and a balanced life quite deliberately; they made it happen. Mine is not of my own making."

Father Martin connected the feeling of torpor with the necessary exercise of purging, a favorite theme. "A lot of purging of the senses is required to cope with torpor," he noted. "There should also be a purging of the mental. One does not feel like focusing on God; it all seems so useless and unfulfilling. I am tempted to throw everything aboard: my faith in God, my hope in eternity, my love of chastity. There is stagnation, depression, and the doldrums."

Father Martin continued to spend more time on this purgative way. "One might not be able to meditate at all. Every attempt to travel to the divine ends in futility. This is spiritual purgation. But don't give up; this can be followed by the illuminative and unitive states. All three stages are part of the mystical journey. Light burns in the soul, a guide more certain than the mid-day sun. Light leads the soul."

"I suppose I experience *acedia* in my own way," Frater Leo reflected during recreation. "I don't sleep well in the morning; consequently, I am sleepy a lot of the time and my life is becoming harder. I feel dry as dust. Events are very repetitive, an unchanging routine, and I feel I am wasting my time.

"But I am told that I am pursued by the noonday demon; I am dying every day but I am living for eternity. I remember praying in a psalm, When will I see the face of God? Am I wrestling with the devil, or like Jacob, with an angel? I often conclude that some people have a gift for this life and others don't. Maybe I am in the last camp.

"But the routine is getting to me: Up at 4:40; prayers at 5 am. Conventual Mass; private masses, serving the Abbot's Mass; breakfast; washing up; preparing readings, class on translating the writings of the Latin Fathers (not Mothers!) of the Church. Sext. Noon meal. The ninth hour for prayer,

None; outside work; meditation in chapel; Vespers; recreation, cards, Matins. Then I recall Pope Leo the Great's words, Christian, remember your dignity. Maybe I am getting closer to God anyway? Still, we're just novices."

Part of the novices' enclosure included sleeping quarters for the four and a connected part with desks, one next to the other. Frater Tobias somehow had a supply of gum and he loved to chew it vigorously, click it and, on occasion, blow bubbles. Frater Jerome wondered how that fit into monastic practice and decorum.

Although Frater Leo was generally well groomed and clean, he had very stinky feet, irritating the nasal passages of Frater Jerome who had a desk nearby; Frater Jerome thought he would gently allude to this dank aroma by telling a joke: "What do you call a monk who walks everywhere in bare, smelly feet, eats a lot of garlic, is extremely weak and has really bad breath? A super-calloused fragile mystic hexed by halitosis." Everyone but Frater Leo was amused at this clever creativity.

EJACULATORY PRAYERS

Monks have many moments during their work or between jobs when they have nothing to do, Father Martin observed. This is a good time to earn merit by way of ejaculations. By uttering simple words and phrases such as Amen, God be praised, Jesus remember me when you come into your kingdom, we elevate our hearts to God. Through these practical and loving remembrances of the presence of God, we guard against inordinate thoughts and actions.

We thereby preserve peace and concord, for religious houses can become veritable hells where each one is the other's devil. Here he recounted St. Paul's First Letter to the Corinthians about love/charity: it is patient, kind, not ambitious, rejoices with the truth and hopes and endures all things. Through these short prayers, we begin to fill our spiritual knapsack.

Father Martin became specific about the time of these prayers of ejaculation: when we wake up in the morning; before beginning any task; at intervals during work, especially when they are very difficult; after the completion of a task; when the clock strikes; when assailed by temptations, melancholy or spiritual dryness; at intervals while pursuing spiritual reading; during times of relaxation; while waiting in line for meals or prayers; during meals.

We can draw these longer or shorter prayers from the Scriptures, especially the psalms. These ferverinos will subdue inordinate cares and purify the imagination from worldly impressions and also lead to helpful actions toward confreres.

Benedictine vows

UNDER FATHER MARTIN'S DIRECTION, we continued to read the *Tyrocinium Benedictinum*, a training manual in monastic life. We were instructed about the temporary vows of three years which could occur after the novitiate. The three vows the Benedictines take are that of stability, or remaining with a chosen house; conversion of manners or morals, including chastity, poverty and renunciation of all possessions; and lastly that of obedience.

He elaborated on each one of the vows, first that of poverty. To demonstrate poverty in possessions, monks put *ad usum*–for the use of–in their books, denoting that they do not own them but were merely using them. In this way, monks were in solidarity with the poor, a good thing.

He pointed to the important place that the poor had in Jewish and Christian Scriptures and our response to them. In the *Book of Leviticus*, God commands Moses: "When you gather the harvest of your land, you are not to harvest to the very end of the field. You are not to gather the gleanings of the harvest. . . You must leave them for the poor and the stranger."

Isaiah writes of a special fast: "to share your bread with the hungry, and shelter the homeless poor, to clothe the man you see to be naked." Father Martin said that even though the monks do not share their food with the hungry, except with students and guests, all people should have at least the spirit of poverty. He pointed to Brother Joe who was overweight and had difficulty walking; this brother said he often fasted, which some did not believe, given his portly frame. In fasting, he said he experienced the plight of the poor and was in solidarity with them. Of course, he could always escape his hungry and thirsty condition, while the really poor could not.

The time of Lent, especially, is a time for this relationship with the starving and dispossessed, and takes the forms of days of fasting, abstinence from meat, and almsgiving. It is a time not just to reduce weight, but, as in the early church, a time to refrain from eating so much and giving either food or the savings from abstinence to the poor. Father Martin said he would talk later about Lent, fasting and abstinence.

"Our fasting is not as extreme as that of the Moslems during their month-long celebration of Ramadan," he said. "For them, this is the time when the prophet Muhammad received the words of the *Koran*. During this month, from dawn to sunset, they don't eat food or drink water and also refrain from sexual activity. Volunteering, performing good works or feeding the poor might be substituted for fasting. But they certainly whoop it up after this period."

In the *Hebrew Testament*, Abraham is a model for sacrificing a portion of the fruit of his labor. He was ready to sacrifice all, in fact, including his son Isaac. After the destruction of the temple in Jerusalem in 70 AD, giving offerings to the poor became a substitute for offerings in the temple. The poor then became the temple.

Of course, Jesus' self-sacrifice on the cross became the foundation for the Christian obligation to give. The poor then become replacements for Jesus. As Jesus in the *Gospel of Matthew* indicates, when you do the works of mercy amid the confusion of our daily lives, we share in God's kingdom; as we practice the works of mercy, helping the least of his brothers and sisters, we do it for the Lord.

Monks abstained from meat on Fridays, just as Catholics around the world were prescribed to do. In the *Ordo,* that book of daily regulations, the original sign for this in Latin was *JM, jejunium monasticae,* a monastic fast. In English it became, MF, monastic fast, or, as the comics said, more food! We took this abstinence or a fast from meat in stride, not reflecting much on our solidarity with the poor.

Father Martin went on to invoke the *Book of Wisdom* in his spin in favor of poverty, at least poverty of spirit. According to the *Book of Proverbs,* practicing poverty or almsgiving will deliver us from death. Giving to the poor is like giving to God who will repay us in full. And in the *Prophet Daniel:* One can pay off the debt of sin by one's charitable acts.

Of course, we have Jesus' astounding words to the rich young man, "Go, sell what you own, give the money to the poor, and you will have treasure in heaven." But giving charitably is not a commercial transaction with God, that is, buying grace and heaven with your good deeds, although God commands us to perform them. We cannot bank up indulgences and therefore gain an eternal reward; Luther poked holes in that type of reasoning.

According to Saints Bonaventure and Augustine, it is God who gives us the grace to be kind, especially to the poor and then God alone deserves the merit or credit. The novice master quoted *The Imitation of Christ:* "The saints do not glory in their own merits, for they attribute no glory to themselves but all to me, because out of my infinite charity I gave all to them."

This approach seemed to contradict what Father Martin had said before about accumulating a lot of merit points. Grace and merit are not commercial ventures.

The act of giving changes the whole person, Father Martin noted, for by giving the giver can see himself and the world in a new light. And from this, the perspective on God also changes, for since God and the poor are so intimately connected, giving to the poor affirms one's belief in God. Again, Father Martin defended the abbey's position for it does not give in an outright fashion, in dollars and cents, to the poor in the district or in the world. But the abbey does give: in its various apostolates, in education at the college, in pastoral work, in the weekly paper and in service through the press.

From my study of Latin and Greek, I came to like the term for poverty, *penuria.* It means penury, that is shortage, scarcity, hardship. But it also means that by having nothing, or little, or just enough, one does not need anything more; one is free of the burden of procuring. Since one does not have any money, one did not accumulate; one has no further need and few worries.

Some monks and professed religious today have a strange idea of poverty, Father Martin said. "They bask in the free services that the communities provide and then do almost nothing for their community inside nor for the community outside. Some of them have their own bank accounts and therefore have a freedom to spend as they wish. But in my day, we were taught that we had to account for every penny we spent. If we were caught with some cash in our pockets when we died, we would be buried on a manure pile."

The monks took the vow of poverty but did not live poorly for, in some way, they were establishment people. They had adequate food, clothing and shelter. They did not have to fret about having enough funds to cover old age and its disabilities. In fact, while they took the vow, often others lived it.

What a life! It was a marvelous turn of events for although the monks had no money, they also had no further needs. True, they could not indulge in many things like going to the movies when they wanted to, buying candy bars on a whim, taking vacations on the beaches and interesting places, although some managed to fit in many such pleasures.

Father Martin said that when some monks travelled, they had a great imagination. They had permission to travel to a certain destination and had funds to make the journey. But they reasoned that, like a candle in really hot weather, their journey could be bent to include other nearby and interesting places.

According to strict rules, monks had to get permission from the abbot to do things that required extended funds. Again, not having money was freeing for one did not have to worry about balancing bank accounts, having enough money for meals, buying car insurance, or clothes. The procurator took care of material needs, and items like toothpaste could be procured from the bookstore.

A lack of money could crimp one's style, however, Father Martin commented. One of the clerics needed to go to town and did not have any money for a bus ride. He had to ask for 50 cents, the round-trip bus fare. He used the first 25 for going to the city, but hitched a ride home, saving 25 cents and returned that amount to the procurator! That was real poverty and a strict interpretation of it.

Monasticism is a kind of socialism, or even communism, at least ideally, with some sense of equality. Monks have most things in common; they provide for one another; their needs are met. According to the early Christian community recalled in the *Acts of the Apostles*, they give according to their ability and receive according to their needs. Monks give without expecting or at least receiving anything in return. If there is profit, it returns to the common coffers. Guests are received without enumerating the costs, although some compensation is appreciated.

"I have focused mostly on the vow of poverty," Father Martin said. "We have already considered the vow of conversion of manners or morals with the *Tyrocinium*, and the vow of obedience is wrapped up in all of these. Now on to the vow of stability.

"Stability is a unique vow for Benedictines. For many religious communities, individuals can be transferred from one house to another, whereas monks stay in the community where they take vows; this is their home; this is where they stay put. So, we don't wander off to find a perfect monastery; we stay with the one we begin with, with the ordinary, a great blessing.

"It is like marriage where there is stability, a commitment to one person to achieve happiness instead of searching for that other perfect person.

It is often tempting to think that we would be happy only if things would change. Instead, through this vow we find happiness in whatever circumstances we encounter. We have a different frame of mind. I am reminded of a saying of one of the desert fathers that when you stay in your cell, your cell will teach you everything.

"So, when we remain constant, wonderful experiences can come our way. Strangely, when we are reliably fixed and present, we can be surprised, receive gifts and grow mentally and spiritually through the ordinary. There is something countercultural here, something old-fashioned.

"Stability can appear to be uncreative and even boring. By staying our whole life with this community, by living together, praying together, working together and relaxing together, we can make advances. When there are personal conflicts, we have to work things out, forgive and restore peace, and our relationships can be strengthened. Whatever work we do, whatever we accomplish, we climb mountains together, advance in wisdom and the spiritual life and rejoice together. Really, stability is a great community vow."

Benedictine medal

FATHER MARTIN BROUGHT INTO the classroom a Benedictine medal for each one of the novices, a gift of Father Abbot. In Scripture, Father Martin explained, St. Peter tells early Christians to be sober and watchful because "your enemy the devil is prowling round like a roaring lion, looking for someone to eat." The devil is real, Father Martin emphasized, "and he wants to destroy all of us through any means possible. So, we have to fight back with the powerful spiritual weapons of prayer and use medals such as this one.

"For centuries the Benedictine medal has been associated with many miracles and has the power of exorcising demons. We do not know the origin of medals but history tells us that in the eleventh century Pope Leo IX attributed his miraculous recovery from a snake bite to a medal.

"At the bottom of this Benedictine medal we read: *ex SM Casino MDCCCLXXX*: from Monte Casino, 1880, a jubilee medal created to commemorate the 1400th anniversary of Benedict's birth.

"I like this medal not only because I am a Benedictine, but because it is rich in meaning. The front contains an image of St. Benedict holding a cross. The cross reminds us of the work of converting and civilizing England and Europe that the Benedictines carried out, especially in the sixth to the ninth/tenth centuries.

"In his left hand, Benedict holds his Rule for monasteries, summed up by his words in the prologue urging monks to walk in God's ways 'with the Gospel for our guide.' On Benedict's left and right are letters stating, 'The cross of our holy father, Benedict.' On a pedestal to his right is a cup with a snake in it; on a pedestal to the left is a raven with some bread.

"The outer edge contains the words in Latin (English), 'May we at our death be fortified by his presence.' Benedict is regarded as the patron of a happy death. Supported by his brothers in the chapel of Monte Cassino, and having received holy communion, Benedict died standing with arms raised to heaven.

"The back of the medal contains the letters *CSPB*, meaning, again, the cross of our holy Father Benedict, and the word *Pax*, peace, at the top. A series of letters on a cross stand for a Latin exorcism prayer, as well as a prayer for guidance:

"*CSSML—NDSMD*, which stand for the rhythmical Latin prayer:

"Crux sacra sit mihi lux!

"Nunquam draco sit mihi dux!

"Translated, it means:

"May the holy cross be my light;

"Let not the dragon be my guide.

"On the outer rim are the letters *VRSNSMV—SMQLIVB*. They stand for another exorcism prayer based on an incident in St. Benedict's life:

"Vade retro Satana!

"Nunquam suade mihi vana!

"Sunt mala quae libas,

"Ipse venena bibas!

"This means:

"Begone, Satan,

"Do not tempt me with your vanities!

"What you offer me is evil.

"Drink the poison yourself!

"Let me give you a short explanation of some of these prayers. After St. Benedict had been a hermit for three years, and his reputation for holiness had spread far and wide, he was asked by a group of monks to be their Abbot. St. Benedict agreed, but some rebellious monks in the community really disliked this idea, and they decided to kill him by poisoning his bread and wine.

"When Benedict made the sign of the cross over his food, as was his custom, he immediately knew that it had been poisoned for a snake emerged from it, the cup shattered and a raven carried away the bread. So, the prayer on the back of the medal refers to Benedict's experience.

"Today, instead of poisoning the abbot to get rid of him, we should be able to vote him out of office, as we do in parliament, but that is not always the case; we can show our displeasure to the regular visitors who ask monks for their suggestions, but the abbot might not comply and might still remain in office for life. But generally, we do not resort to assassination by poison or by any other means.

"There is no specific way to carry or wear the medal," Father Martin said. "You can wear it on a chain around your neck, attach it to your rosary or keep it in your pocket. Some lay people bury it in the foundation of their homes, place it in their workplaces or even in their barns. In all these places, the medal through the intercession of Benedict, can call down God's blessing and protection. It can become a constant silent prayer reminding us that we are followers of Christ. It is an arsenal, like a bullet-proof vest, a sacramental."

It was obvious that Father Martin was sold on the medal, for he continued: "It is a prayer of exorcism against the devil, a prayer for strength during temptation and for peace here and everywhere.

"We should study those inscriptions and think about the lessons they contain. This medal can be a constant reminder of our need to take up the cross daily and follow 'the true King, Christ the Lord' and thus learn 'to share in his kingdom,' as St. Benedict urges us in the prologue of his Rule."

Art and monastic life

ORDINARILY FATHER MARTIN WAS not given to artistic displays or esthetic musings. But this time he brought into the classroom an art book from the library featuring five reproductions by Jean-François Millet. Farming and relative poverty were experiences both Father Martin and Jean-François shared. At first, the Parisian salons regarded the painter's works as crude and unfinished, but they had to admit that he demonstrated a love of the soil; although his characters lived in poverty, they displayed a great dignity.

"I remember seeing in grade school a copy of Millet's painting on The Reapers. Our school thought it was a nice work because if showed farmers toiling and we were farmers used to stooking our grain," Frater Tobias said.

Father Martin pointed out that in another painting, The Gleaners, Millet exposes the ancient practice and obligation not to reap the wasted stalks of grain in the expansive areas nor to cut the stems in the corners. When these were left uncut, the poor were invited to glean these stray stalks. Millet depicted not the rich in their fancy garbs but the country folk in their simple apparel. However, they do not pose in demeaning positions; instead, they are models to imitate.

The Gleaners presents three peasant women stooped over to gather the last scraps of a harvest. Their obscured faces in semi-darkness blend into the hushed background. These haunting figures work in contrast to the rich folk at the top of the painting. The gleaners seem fixed, not upwardly mobile in their dependency.

Millet contrasts the scavenging women and the wealthy, the vulnerable and the powerful, and female and male. The poor and powerless are clothed in simple, greyish garments, in contrast to the rich with their horses, giant haystacks, and well-developed farmyard.

"A golden light evokes the sacred and the long-lasting," Father Martin said. "Peasant life has nobility, is worthwhile and holy despite its back-breaking and repetitious labor. With their homespun dresses set against the golden field, these women are resolute and tough."

Another of Millet's paintings, Faggot Gatherers Returning from the Forest, brought sad memories to Frater Tobias. He remembers his grandfather telling him that as a child he gathered wood from the Hungarian forest for his family. "One time an overlord on horseback intercepted him as he was carrying heavy bundles and whipped him. A similar boss might ride up unexpectedly and whip these old women."

"Those who are faceless and hunched over remind me of my peasant ancestors," Father Martin said. "The female figures meld into each other, becoming faceless, with the one in front separated from the rest and hidden by the bundles. The forest envelopes these human bodies, becoming one with them as the figures become one with the forest."

Two representations are entitled, The Sower. In the first, the farmer melds with a harrower, a flock of crows, and a barely visible tower. The sower is excited and carefree in his work. He believes the soil will produce an abundant crop as he swings his arms and dances with great confidence. But he is also a planner, for he covers the seeds before the birds eat them.

Father Martin also referred to Jesus' parable of the sower in the Gospel. In this second painting, the sower is life-sized and powerful, trudges along the pliable earth, eagerly and forcefully thrusting the grain from his calloused hand. He is a colorful, muscular figure with rough weather-worn skin. This sower is intent on his job even though his hat hides his face. He is making plans as he looks into the distance. Bathed in the sun's warming light, he is not just any old peasant; he is not lazy but advances methodically even as the day completes its cycle.

Millet's last reproduction to be considered is The Angelus. Two figures respond to the Angelus bell ringing three times a day, morning, noon and evening, a signing of the day as in monastic life. For these peasants, the church bell keeps time for them, marking periods to pause, repeat the words of the angel, Gabriel, and recite the Hail Marys.

While the bell rings, the two figures stop their digging of potatoes, and abandon their use of garden tools. They welcome the bell; it is a time to pray, to be with God. This painting radiates peace and simplicity. There is no fuss as white light surrounds the peasants and a warm sun sets on the horizon. Millet's young man removes his hat, holds it in his hands, swaddles it on his chest, and bows his head. The young girl places her hands near her face, also bows her head and recites her prayers.

Antiquarian nature of the monastery

As WE WERE HOEING the weeds around the apple trees in the monastic orchard, we could hear the farm manager, a rather aged monk, using a tractor to pull a binder out of the machine shed.

While those of us from farms could remember using these binders to cut and bundle grain into sheaves, this practice had more or less been phased out on area farms. I remember the garden manager rather sheepishly referring to this farm operation and justifying it since there were quite a few young monks available to do this hands-on work. These readily available monks could easily put the sheaves into stooks, an operation regarded as very work intensive for today's modern farmers.

Many of us regarded the hoeing of the evergreen trees and those in the orchard as make-work projects. They were not that laborious and they provided an occasion for great camaraderie, but surely these was a more modern way of getting rid of weeds! In fact, the orchard manager himself demonstrated this as he wielded his Minneapolis Z tractor and its harrow-toothed cultivator through the larger expanses of the orchard and the grove of pine trees. Why not use this technique to get closer to the trees and do away with the need for hand hoeing?

With his farming background, Frater Tobias thought that hoeing was a rather primitive way of eradicating weeds. In his farm experience, he used a tractor and cultivator to get rid of these prairie pests. His father used chemical spray on the fields. Instead, novices now were involved in what the novice master called, *utilis occupatio*, useful work, but also work to fill in unoccupied time. Some of us called it useless work. But in this monastery, there were abundant personnel and time for a less efficient way of doing things and hoeing was one of them.

The novices had experienced the ready availability of hot and cold running water in their homes, and also indoor toilets with sewer systems. In the monastery, however, there was only one washroom and novices could theoretically wash there but were encouraged, in the old fashion, to use a large porcelain pitcher to procure water for their own bedroom, and then use that in a large wash basin. Such a private procedure kept the novices away from an interchange with other monks in the bathroom, but it seemed like a very antiquated ritual for washing in the morning.

Praying in Latin was a challenge. First of all, it was not our native language although the Mass was in Latin and some of us remembered the readings in our parishes, first in Latin, then in English or German. But in the monastery, we read and listened to commentaries by the Fathers of the Church in Latin. All our monastic prayers and the public daily chanting of the martyrology were in Latin.

Some of us did a little spiritual reading in Greek, that is, reading from the Greek *New Testament*. We had studied mostly classical Greek and this *koine* or common Greek of the Bible was a little different from the classical form. While reading the Greek, we had to cheat a little and check the English or Latin translation to make sure we understood what was written.

In high school we learned to depend on bells to remind us when to wake up–really a time for bells and smells–times for the beginning of classes and the end of them, times for study hall. However, it still seemed a little unusual to have one's life regulated almost entirely in this fashion. Nevertheless, if one relied on bells to regulate one's life, one did not have to take the initiative to begin and conclude tasks for it all depended on the bells telling us to keep the schedule; it was part of the rules we had to keep. While some hated the bell regulators, others welcomed them; they removed some tension from life; they did not make us dependent on our own willfulness; they helped us make decisions; they solved the dilemma about what to do with one's life.

One of my fellow novices welcomed such an ordering and even adored it. He had smuggled an alarm clock into the novitiate, and while he did not set its alarm, he checked it during the night to make sure he did not miss the regular bell in the morning. I thought that such an approach bordered on fanaticism. I needed my sleep and detested that bell. I wanted to allow myself some leeway both during the night and during the day. I did not want to be devoted slavishly to any programing.

Before one of his classes, Father Martin singled out Frater Jerome for a private talk. He told him of his concern, and that of the Abbot, that Frater Jerome had not taken classes in the Greek language during his year of college. "This is a grave omission," Father Martin said, "because clerics studying for the priesthood must be able to read and examine the *New Testament* writings in the original. Without a knowledge of Greek and further study in it, that is not possible. However, the rule for novices is that they do no academic work during their novitiate.

"But in your case, we have to make an exception. You will study Greek with Frater Tobias and will take the university exam. Then you will be able to take upper year classes in the Greek language after the novitiate is over." Frater Jerome began studying from a textbook with Frater Tobias but found the process tedious and so they mutually agreed that Frater Jerome would continue to study by himself, which he did and then took the final exam and passed, triumphantly.

ORDINARY TASKS

Monks shared the chores necessary to keep the monastery running smoothly. One worked in a dry goods store previously and had some experience in tailoring; he measured the habits for the novices and other monks. Another was a bookphile and he became librarian, catalogued the books, and bound the periodicals. During harvest time the call came for additional help in the garden and in the fields; even the editor of the provincial paper donned his overalls in the afternoon to share in stooking the sheaves.

Whenever monks needed a haircut, there was always someone who could do the job; during Easter time and Christmas celebrations, and when the students were on holidays, monks went to the parishes to hear confessions, celebrate the liturgy and keep fellow monks company; when there were vacancies among the teaching staff, monks were selected to receive additional training to fill these positions, often done regardless of their specific talents or preferences.

"The strength of the monastery is to keep its traditions and guard its treasures," Father Martin stated. "The Benedictine legacy is to pray and to work. In these ways we experience God in ordinary life. Dozens of small routine tasks can lead to extraordinary experiences of God."

"I remember hearing about the call of God as some kind of seduction," Frater Leo remembered. "I was kind of enchanted, foolish enough to give up my material possessions and join the monastery. But what really fascinated me was the dedication of the monks in the boys' boarding school. They were always available for us, whether in the dormitory, the chapel, the refectory, classroom or playground.

"They also formed a community which I wanted to join. Everything that they did was good for their souls and for our souls. Even when some of us misbehaved, we were corrected with fairness. These monks had a sense of purpose. They persevered and did not give up."

Father Martin became quite romantic and idyllic in his next remarks. In a spirited fashion he recalled some of his ordinary experiences which he deemed extraordinary. "The stars, the endless landscapes, and the clouds are enrapturing; they speak of their immensity. The changing seasons of the year, winter's melting icicles and spring flowers and summer sun, give excitement and glee. In such raptures, one senses the presence of God and cannot fear death but can even look forward to it. In some way, everything, even tragedies and setbacks, can be good for the soul.

"The monastic life is a deep search for meaning. Although we are fragmented, unfinished saints, people living within these walls are truly free and those on the outside are more like prisoners. In this monastic enclosure, we can experience a wonderful stillness and a complete sense of purpose. Our simple robes are more dignified than the expensive clothing of the rich. Ours is an inner wealth."

"But I keep searching. Can I forego all that the world offers, close myself off forever within these stone walls and search for God while awaiting death under the same routine for decades?" Frater Leo continued to question.

HELL LIBRARY

Novices began to feel that there were a lot of prohibitions for them and also for other monks. One of these restrictions pertained to the library.

There was a section of the monastic library which contained books on the Index, that is, those included on the List of Prohibited Books. The monks called it the hell library. Seasoned monks were cautioned to use this part of the library only for serious research and generally should check its usage with their superior or spiritual adviser.

The door to the hell library was locked but it was known that the key was kept in the librarian's desk and so quite accessible for those with a little cunning. The hell library was an intriguing area especially because it was a forbidden domain. The volumes it contained were censored or deemed heretical by the Roman Catholic church in order to protect the faith and morals of the faithful. To ensure this protection, church authorities prevented the reading of theologically, culturally, or politically disruptive books. The titles were censored therefore for various reasons such as heresy, moral deficiency or sexual explicitness.

To provide a more positive guide as to whether books were safe for Catholics, proper reading materials included a *nihil obstat* (nothing forbids) notation at the beginning of a book, given by the local bishop, or the designation, *imprimatur* (it can be printed). These signs indicated a judgment that such books were safe on matters of faith and morals.

Unlike the past, church authorities today no longer proclaimed or enacted the death of individuals for writing or reading prohibited material. Also, they no longer burned such books but merely stored them in a restricted place.

Two brash novices inquired of the librarian which books might be on this Index based on a list they provided him. While the monk librarian was forthright in indicating which were forbidden, he was surprised and found it strange that novices were knowledgeable about such titles given the explicit sexual content of some of them.

These titles included *Lady Chatterley's Lover* by D. H. Lawrence, *Brave New World* by Aldous Huxley, *Mein Kampf* by Adolph Hitler, *Lolita* by Vladimir Nabokov, *The Catcher in the Rye* by J. D. Salinger, *Being and Nothingness* by Jean-Paul Sartre, and a few works by the Jesuit priest, Pierre Teilhard de Chardin.

"Of course, you have to have serious reasons for reading these works and have to get permission," the librarian cautioned.

Frater Tobias was fascinated by the name hell library, but also curious about its meaning. He could understand that it was the repository of evil books and therefore merited the name hell. Hellish books were there just as hell was a place to which evildoers were consigned. But was one doomed to hell if one read these books, at least without special permission? This possibility did not stop him from trying to snoop around this library.

While he was studying the French language in order to teach it, Father Martin confessed that he had read about a novel from Montreal by Jean-Charles Harvey, *Les Demi-civilisés*. It was controversial all right, but he thought he would like to read it to increase his knowledge of the language and French-Canadian culture. However, it was on the Index of Prohibited Books.

"I was anxious to read it, maybe because of its prohibition," he admitted sheepishly, "so I sought and received permission from the Abbot. I read reviews of the book and found out that Cardinal Jean-Marie-Rodrique Villeneuve, archbishop of Quebec, had placed it on the Index citing Canon Law which called for the banning of works that 'purposely attack religion or good morals.'

"This prohibition made the novel very popular; however, it did not attack religion or good morals but the church where the half-civilized were the clergy, politicians and businessmen. One of the characters in the novel takes pride in reading books on the Index surreptitiously; he confides that the prohibition enticed him to do so. The upshot was that the novel became hot stuff and was soon out of print. But no rue, no street was named after Harvey!

"I enjoyed Harvey's satire against the bourgeois elite and the suffocating rule of the Catholic clergy. No wonder it created such a furor in Quebec. It also lampooned politics, manners and education and advocated a strong, free and independent nation of civilized people springing from the virtues of peasants. No immorality here, but my eyes were opened about Quebec, past and present; no wonder the book was condemned!" Father Martin concluded.

GETTING A BLESSING

The novices seldom left the monastic grounds but Frater Tobias got up his nerve to do so when his grandmother died and was being buried in a neighboring parish cemetery. He made the case, not informed by monastic norms, that he was close to her and actually stayed on his grandparent's farm during a fall and wintertime when his parents went to Toronto to work. Therefore, he should be given permission to attend the funeral.

Since a priest was leaving the monastery for that parish in the morning, Frater Tobias could catch a ride with him. The Abbot gave his approval reluctantly and informed Novice Tobias that he was to be back in time for evening prayers. The ritual for such a departure included getting a blessing from Father Abbot, following a directive in the Rule which stated that a junior should ask the senior for a blessing. So, Frater Tobias knelt down and asked the Abbot's blessing and departed.

Frater Tobias' parents, especially his mother, were delighted he could come for this occasion. In the parish, he was the center of attention and curiosity, especially after the funeral ritual and during its reception. In his conspicuous, long, black robe, he moved from handshake to handshake with his many cousins, aunts and uncles. He relished all the fuss.

As the lunch time passed, however, Frater Tobias remembered the deadline he had–return for Matins. His parents suggested that his cousins who were of the same age could transport him there. He approached them and they readily agreed; he rounded up five, which took some time for they were in no great hurry to head to the abbey. As they drove, Frater Tobias checked his watch several times and grew more and more apprehensive about the stringent ruling on punctuality.

In the car, they had a great time sharing their many mutual experiences. At Frater Tobias' encouragement and insistence, cousin Fabian drove with considerable speed and made it to the abbey grounds just as the clock turned 7:30. Frater Tobias bade them a quick farewell and thank you, realizing that such a deadline was a mystery to them. He made it into the chapel just as the Matins prayer began. Whew!

About two weeks after I returned from my grandma's funeral, I began to have a fever and my eyes turned red. My body was aching and I had a sore throat. I went to Father Martin and he immediately led me to a vacant room in the monastery for a period of isolation. He closed the drapes on the windows and brought me my Bible, a book of psalms, and some spiritual reading I had already begun.

After a few days I got a rash over my face and on the rest of my body. I did not feel like reading for my eyes were very sore. I was diagnosed with measles which I must have picked up at my grandma's funeral. At first, my appetite was down, and for a week each of my novice confreres in turn was deputed to bring me my meals on a tray. After they put it near my bed, they withdrew some distance so as not to be contaminated. I was grateful for their service and presence and the conversation about what I was missing in the novitiate. As it was, the three who brought me my meals also came down with measles. It was a noble sacrifice on their part.

The liturgical year

ADVENT

CHRISTMAS IN THE MONASTERY was a little different. The monks were liturgically correct by not letting Christmas make its appearance too soon. First, there were the four Sundays of Advent before Christmas, a time when we prepared for the Messiah by praying the words and images of John the Baptist and Mary. John the Baptist was an intriguing figure with stringy hair and the strange habit of eating locusts.

"Would we welcome such a filthy guy into the monastery," I wondered. "He railed against those who were rule bound and self-righteous and called them a brood of vipers. Are we monks a brood of vipers? Do his words include us?"

During the latter days of Advent, we were introduced to the O Antiphons. These were sung or recited during the last seven days of Advent and began the Vesper canticle, *Magnificat,* a chanted section, from Dec. 17 to Dec. 23. They are referred to as the Os because the title of each one begins with the letter O and is a name for Christ, his characteristics mentioned in Scripture. While the monks generally recited them, we appreciated when Father Daniel sang them so beautifully during the Office.

Father Martin suggested that during this part of Advent the novices meditate on the meaning of these antiphons as they appeared. "In some fashion these O Antiphons have been part of the liturgical tradition since the early church," he said. "Likely, these antiphons date from the sixth century and Boethius refers to them in *The Consolation of Philosophy.*

"There is a twofold importance to the O Antiphons. First, each one is a title for the Messiah. Second, each one refers to the prophecy of Isaiah about the coming of the Messiah. The first antiphon is O *Sapientia:* 'O

Wisdom, reaching from one end to the other, mightily and sweetly order-ing all things: Come and teach us the way of prudence.' It is a compilation of various texts from the *Prophet Isaiah, Sirach, Wisdom of Solomon* and the *Gospel of John.*

"The second one is *O Adonai,* the highest possible sovereign: 'O Ado-nai, and leader of the House of Israel, who appeared to Moses in the fire of the burning bush and gave him the law on Sinai: Come and redeem us with an outstretched arm.' The words are from Isaiah and the *Book of Exodus.*

"The next ones are *O Radix Jesse,* O Root of Jesse; *O Clavis,* O Key of David; *O Oriens,* O Morning Star; *O Rex Gentium,* O King of the Nations; the last is 'O Emmanuel [God is with us], our king and our lawgiver, the hope of the nations and their Saviour: Come and save us, O Lord our God.'

"Isaiah had prophesied as follows," Father Martin said: "Therefore, the Lord himself will give you a sign. Look, the young woman is with child and shall bear a son, and shall name him Immanuel.'

"In some monasteries the monks make a large wreath for each of these O Antiphons, append on it the initial words of each one and arrange them in conspicuous places outside the monastery."

He also noted an interesting but a not-so-reliable detail: early monks arranged these antiphons in such a way that their first letters translate into *Ero cras,* "Tomorrow, I will be there," supposedly mirroring the meaning of the antiphons leading to Jesus' coming at Christmas. Thus, beginning with the last one, *Emmanuel,* then the following first letters, not really in order, *Rex, Oriens, Clavis, Radix, Adonai,* and *Sapientia,* giving *Ero cras.* "But there is little support that the monks intended this more arcane arrange-ment for there is no cryptic message in the O Antiphons," Father Martin concluded.

CHRISTMAS

Just before Christmas day, some Brothers felled a tall evergreen tree from the nursery and erected it in the chapel. They decorated it with shiny balls, candles and candy canes. A large star on top gave the tree extra prominence.

My first midnight Mass in the monastery was quite different from that in our rural setting. In both places we celebrated at midnight because Jesus was believed to have been born at this time. In the monastery we gathered in the chapel a half hour before Mass; monks of German extraction and others sang German carols of which I remember especially, *Stille Nacht, heilige Nacht,* Silent Night, Holy Night, sung just before midnight.

Father Abbot, celebrated the Mass with his golden vestments assisted by a deacon and subdeacon. Incense wafted above, the organ was louder, the singing more exuberant. The readings spoke of light that shines for there is a lot of darkness around us. This new event surprises both the angels and shepherds for God meets us, visits us with his Son, takes us by the hand.

Monastic Christmas was moving, but I really missed the opening of presents at home when we returned from midnight Mass and I also missed eating "Jap" oranges, lots of poppy bread and drinking warm cocoa. But no eating here.

While we novices were not permitted to correspond regularly with anyone during the novitiate, not even with members of our families, we were told to write to our mothers and fathers in early December, and suggest that they visit on Christmas day or shortly thereafter for a period of an hour or so. Frater Tobias eagerly and dutifully did so and his parents and siblings indicated they would be present on Christmas day.

On their arrival, the family proceeded to the visitors' room. Frater Tobias' siblings brought along a chocolate treat and also displayed some of the presents they received. His brothers and sister each got a new pair of skates ordered from Eaton's catalogue. They eagerly shared the news that they had cleared the snow from a portion of their nearby lake, and had now tried to skate, supported by their hockey sticks. In early December, they had already played a lot of foot hockey at school, sometimes using horse turds instead of pucks.

Frater Tobias' parents noted that their parents had tried to recreate the first Christmas by putting hay under the table to imitate the manger in the stable. Mom and Dad shared news of relatives, the opportunities they had taken or forsaken, the deaths, births and marriages. In keeping with monastic practice, Frater Tobias did not have any food or gifts to share and the family understood this. The hour elapsed quickly and he bade them a fond but reluctant farewell.

Strangely, during the Christmas season Frater Tobias remembered his 4-H days during which he, with the agricultural club members, toured the Prince Albert Penitentiary. He was very young and had forgotten much of the experience, but today he wondered how come the Club had chosen such a destination. It was important for the early Prince Albert residents to have such a facility; it was a third- place selection for the province; Regina got first with the Parliament, and Saskatoon, second, with the University.

Frater Tobias' memory was stirred when he read an item in the *Prairie Messenger* under the heading, Inside the Walls. David recalled on the front page of the *Messenger* his experience of Christmas in the pen. He measured this internal experience with his previous external ones in his home before his incarceration.

David was a young man who had never been in jail before and was apprehensive about this new experience beginning in October, shortly after harvest time. He was a simple farm boy and had heard stories of first-time inmates being robbed, assaulted and raped. As he entered his cell, he could sense the inmates' suspicious glances for they did not seem to trust anyone who did not share their mindless destructiveness, their anger and paranoia.

But here it was Christmas time and David had survived so far with little trauma. In fact, he had made a few friends.

"I got a few Christmas notes from fellow prisoners and also letters and cards from my family," David wrote, "although these were thoroughly inspected lest they be soaked in dopey substances." He hoped to phone his family on this day, as he did every week, but this was a busy time and there were too many people lined up to use the phone. "Maybe the prison system wanted you to be disconnected during this festive time?" he questioned.

"I had extra money and so I bought some canteen stuff, junk food really, but it helped celebrate a little. Not like the pig in the blanket, Christmas cake and jelly salad that I had at home."

Compared to his family standards, the food on Christmas day was about the same as usual this time, that is, terrible. But maybe a little better than the regular fare of a few cold-cuts, some cheese, a rather stale hotdog bun, a bit of a peach, and some queer tasting soup. This time there was some processed turkey, salty stuffing and instant potatoes. "Since the PA Pen had a farm, you would think they could do better than that!" David penned.

"We stayed in our cells longer than usual since some of the guards were on holidays, which is fair enough, and so there was not sufficient staff to supervise us. They were operating on a shoe string. So, no visits with relatives and friends during the holidays. But this schedule could lead to more suicides and fights.

"I was beginning to feel really sorry for myself," David continued. "I thought of my family. They were also suffering from my imprisonment. In regular conversations with neighbors and relatives, they did not mention my name very often, if at all. At dinner table, they set an empty plate for me, which was nice. However, I felt through my absence that I did not share responsibility in their tasks. Christmas time is when we prisoners are most affected since we are away from our loved ones and are consigned to be mostly by ourselves. When I thought of everything, I was full of pain and felt forgotten; I cried myself to sleep.

"The next days were a little more jovial. Before they left for their holidays, the guards had organized ping pong and pool tournaments. All of us signed up, even those who were poor players. The winners got $2 in canteen credit. We realized it was a time to keep us occupied but we appreciated it."

"I got a little down remembering that prison story and had to shake myself up to recall the previous glorious night," Frater Tobias recounted. "One of the memorable readings during Christmas Matins was from Pope Leo the Great in the fifth century, a passage Frater Leo had quoted briefly when he gave his report on his patron saint. Even in Latin I could feel its importance and so here it is:

"Agnoce, O Christiane, dignitatem tuam, et divinae consors factus naturae, noli in veterem vilitatem degeneri conversatione redire. Memento, cujus capitis et cujus corporis sis membrum. Reminiscere, quia erutus de potestate tenebrarum, translatus es in Dei lumen et regnum.

"Christian, recognize your dignity! Since you now share in the divine nature, do not return to your former base condition by unworthy conduct. Remember Who is your Head and of Whose Body you are a member. Never forget that you have been rescued from the power of darkness and brought into the light of the Kingdom of God."

"After the pomp of midnight Mass, here I am alone in my cell, not exactly a prison cell, and thinking of the meaning of Christmas. One part of me is filled with the rapture of the event. The other part is my memory of the past, which we were told not to do.

"I recalled that the winter air on the farm had a bite, snowflakes dancing lightly above, hovering and not reaching the ground immediately. Darkness came quickly, wrapped itself around me, pushed me indoors into its warmth and light. My Mom turned up the heat and put the kettle on.

"One of the most romantic experiences on the farm was our trek by horse and caboose to our church for midnight Christmas Mass. While a full moon often guided our horses along the packed ice and snow road, Dad did not rely on the moon alone to guide us. He placed our wet cell car battery behind the back seat of the caboose and stretched a wire to a global tractor light affixed to the roof. This provided an illuminating beam between the horses and onto the road in front of them. As the horses trotted along, they spewed rising steam in the flickering light.

"We could see the wondrous stars, just as the Three Kings followed one of them, and occasionally viewed the northern lights, quite a celestial event. We had a panoramic view of the very dark night sky, since Dec. 24 was nearly the longest night of the year.

"Although we sometimes felt a tinge of nocturnal nervousness, we knew animals were near, such as bush rabbits hiding in the snow's relative warm cover, prairie chickens hovering together, and coyotes howling to us and to one another. A poet noted that those who braved the dark had stellar experiences–the sounds of feuding, feeding and fornicating creatures. Once at home again, we trekked by foot through the crunchy snow from the caboose and barn to our house."

LENT

St. Benedict's Rule has a short chapter on the observance of Lent. He posts a directive for this period of time: looking "forward to holy Easter with joy and spiritual longing." For Frater Callistus, the forty days of Lent were a mystical number like Ali Baba and the forty thieves. The Rule, however, stated that the forty days should be a period of *metanoia*, conversion, recalling the forty years Moses spent in the desert with his people and the hours Jesus spent in prayer.

For Lent, the Rule states that the monk should "deny himself some food, drink, sleep, needless talking and idle jesting." Frater Tobias confessed that refraining from food and drink before morning communion already made him weak and sick to his stomach.

The acting novice master asked each novice to present him with a list of actions for this period. He reminded them that the Rule prescribes that during Lent each monk shall "receive a book from the library, and is to read the whole of it straight through." The novice master took up this precept and suggested we read the lives of the saints and those who had a reputation for holiness, such as Benedict Labre, although he confessed that dressing in his shabby way, not taking baths and pushing insects back into his sleeve might not be something to be imitated.

Along liturgical lines, he recommended we read the writings of Pius Parsch, *The Church's Year of Grace*, especially his comments on Lent and Easter. Then there is Reginald Garrigou-Lagrange, John Cassian, and *The Psalms are Christian Prayer* by Thomas Worden; Thomas Merton's *Seven Storey Mountain*; Vicktor Frankl's *Man's Search for Meaning*. Father Martin examined each of our Lenten lists and made his own suggestions, based presumably on what he knew about us and what might be a good individual penance.

The monks abstained from meat on Fridays during the year, just as Catholics around the world were prescribed to do. We took this abstinence or a fast from meat in stride, not reflecting much on our solidarity with the poor.

I really hated waiting for food especially for such a long period in the morning, and also found it hard not to drink anything. I had been diagnosed with the condition of mucus colitis and my stomach burned when empty for a long time. I was too shy and embarrassed to ask for an exemption from these rules, however.

My Dad said that there were always exceptions to every rule. In this case, he gave the example of his brother who served in the army during World War II. Because of the tension and energy required to prepare for and engage in combat, they were freed from this observance of fasting and some even took the liberty of eating meat on Fridays, especially when there was no fish available or they needed extra strength. Dad also pointed out that some of the returning soldiers thought this exception to the rule prevailed even after their discharge and so they did not observe fasting and abstinence. For Dad this was a humorous interpretation.

Although Germans in our rural community were known for being law abiding, there was some who found loopholes in Catholic obligations, particularly in keeping the Sunday work-free. One farmer argued that on the basis that God/Yahweh worked for six days and then rested, humans could do the same. So, if one works three days and it rained, then one could work an additional three days, making six in total. But if the additional three days included Sunday, then one could work on Sunday and thereby keep the same timetable as God!

Father Martin pointed to themes during Lent, beginning with the Third Sunday. In the Gospel reading for this Sunday, Jesus meets a Samaritan woman at Jacob's well. Besides crossing racial lines, for Jews and Samaritans hated each other, Jesus singles out water as being very important in life and that he is the fulfillment of the prophets and the source of living water.

Of course, water at baptism is central to mid-eastern life. The Garden of Eden was watered by a stream; the journeys of the patriarchs and their families led them from well to well, for watering sites were places of meeting in an arid land. These people expected God to provide water as a gift to them.

We can discover new perspectives in this scene of the Samaritan woman, Father Martin said. Jesus, a weary man, asks her for a drink. Her encounter with Jesus drew many fellow Samaritans to him. This focus on water points to living water as a sign of messianic gifts, for John's Gospel is not merely a news item; those who drink earthly waters, will thirst again, but those who drink these waters will never thirst again.

The next Sunday of Lent focused on light and the man born blind. John's Gospel begins by stating that the coming of God's Word into the world is a light which overcomes darkness and enlightens everyone. Jesus is this word from the Father which enlightens the world; in the Gospel, Jesus applies a little mud to the man's eyes, commands him to wash in the Pool of Siloam and then he sees.

Little by little his inner eyes are also opened and he believes. This reading foreshadows for catechumens, those preparing for baptism, the waters of initiation at Easter time. Like the blind man, the newly baptized engage in a marvelous transformation from darkness to light.

And in the Gospel for the next Sunday, Lazarus is raised from the dead. For the Gospel writer, St. John, the raising of Lazarus is the last sign that Jesus works in order to manifest the glory of the Father. These signs and actions tell us who Jesus is; they point to his suffering on the cross and the elevation of the Son of Man. From his side gushes blood and water, signs of the fecundity of Christ's death.

Lazarus helps us to understand the meaning of the Lord's passion. His hour has come and Jesus assures Martha that her brother will come back to life. However, he is perturbed and deeply troubled and weeps. "See how much he loved him," the Jews said. "He opened the eyes of the blind man, could he not have prevented this man's death?"

The calling of Lazarus back to life for a while prefigures Jesus' triumph on the cross. Believers pass to the life that bodily death cannot touch. That process of moving toward life is started at baptism in which we are born to faith but still have to make those inescapable steps of suffering and death.

"Lent is a time to reflect on the past twelve months with a view to changing what is necessary," Father Martin commented. "That is what conversion or *metanoia* is all about. It might mean taking the fasting and abstinence a little more seriously; in the Lenten fast, breakfast and lunch should not equal more in quantity than supper. The *Tyrocinium* observes that obviously intoxication and gluttony are to be avoided because they lead to lust."

During Lent, statues, crucifixes and paintings were veiled in purple. In the liturgical ceremonies, the sound of dry clappers replaced those of bells.

At mid-Lent there is a respite from the regimen of fasting and abstinence and this is indicated during the Sunday service when the word, *Laetare*, Rejoice, begins the Mass. It is a breather from austerity, a taste of joy during seriousness, shown by rose-colored vestments in the liturgy and dumplings for dinner.

Things get more serious again with Passion Sunday. Events, however, did not remain morose for long; during Palm/Passion Sunday there were signs of joy: a procession with the waving of palms, singing *Hosanna,* and rejoicing with a view to the celebration of the resurrection.

We got the feeling that there was something special coming up because of the upbeat spirit of the psalms and readings during our prayers. But this spirit was ushered in gradually, beginning with a *Tenebrae* ceremony in the Divine Office, a shadow or darkness service, during which candles were progressively extinguished.

THE *TRIDUUM,* THE THREE DAYS

I remember that day before Easter Sunday, Maundy Thursday, Holy Thursday, when Father Daniel sang so splendidly from the *Lamentations of Jeremiah.* It is from an ancient chant melody. The Hebrew alphabet, *Aleph, Beth,* etc., prefaced each verse. During Mass, Father Abbot washed the feet of several monks. Since I was selected for the washing, I had to cut my toenails and clean my feet.

This ceremony followed the compelling example of Jesus' washing his disciples' feet at the Last Supper. At the end of this liturgical celebration, the Abbot processed with the ciborium, containing the hosts, to the side altar. The main altar was stripped of its linen, the tabernacle now empty, with its doors flung open. This marked the beginning of the Three Days, the *Triduum.*

I noticed that for the afternoon Good Friday service, there were no decorations of any kind. This celebration sometimes coincided with the Jewish observance of Passover. It was a civic holiday with a minimum of shopping, a day of fasting and abstinence from meat.

The first part of the liturgy was the adoration of the cross. It was unveiled and then Father Abbot with assistants silently entered the chapel, prostrated themselves before the altar in humility and sorrow. There were readings from the *Prophet Isaiah,* the *Book of Hebrews* and the passion account of St. John.

For the second part of the liturgy, there were solemn intercessions with prayers for the Pope, clergy and laity, those preparing for baptism, for the unity of Christians, the Jewish people, those who do not believe in Christ and those who do not believe in God, those in public office and those who have special needs. After each intention, the deacon bade the faithful kneel for a short prayer, and the celebrant summed up the prayer intention.

Next followed the unveiling and adoration of the cross. All present venerated it by kissing it. Next, holy communion beginning with the recitation of the Our Father in Latin. The presider then departed in silence.

EASTER

For the evening vigil ceremony on Saturday night, Father Abbot inserted grains of incense into five openings in the tall Easter candle, indicating the five wounds of Jesus. He also inscribed on the candle the date of the civic year. After this paschal candle was lit, the deacon lifted it high and processed into the church with the refrain, *Lumen Christi,* Light of Christ; he intoned it three times with each phrase on a higher pitch. New light from this main candle spread from person to person, from candle to candle until the chapel was aglow with its light. Like churches around the world, there was new light, new joy, fresh hope.

Father Daniel sang the *Exsultet,* the glorious Easter hymn of praise, in front of the paschal candle, chanting the sublime proclamation: "Rejoice, heavenly powers! Sing, choirs of angels! Exult, all creation around God's throne! Jesus Christ, our King, is risen! Sound the trumpet of salvation! . . . This is the night when Jesus Christ broke the chains of death and rose triumphant from the grave. . . O happy fault, O necessary sin of Adam, which gained for us so great a Redeemer!"

The Liturgy of the Word was next, consisting of nine readings from the Bible telling of the beginning of salvation, all a foreshadowing of baptism and resurrection. Then the altar candles were lit, new linen spread on the altar, lilies in full bloom placed around the altar, the jubilant *Gloria in Excelsis Deo* intoned, bells rung, every stop on the organ open, every voice joined in the triumphant response.

During the baptismal rite, the Easter candle was inserted into the font three times. Father Martin had indicated to us that at this time in the ancient church, the catechumens were baptized. Then followed the renewal of baptismal vows.

We celebrated the Spirit's presence during 50 days of Easter and especially at Pentecost when the Holy Spirit came down on the fearful group in the upper room. We had a special Pontifical Mass with the Abbot celebrating and the Prior preaching.

"What joyful, moving celebrations!" Frater Jerome said.

"For me this is a time of new life," Frater Tobias reflected. "On the farm, I saw many calves emerge from the womb. These were joyous occasions, moments to celebrate as we do at Easter."

ROAD TO EMMAUS

In one of his talks, Father Martin announced that on the day after Easter Sunday, that is, Easter Monday, he and the novices, like Jesus' disciples, would take an extended walk. This walk would be like the one Jesus took with his immediate followers on the way to Emmaus, except we would not be like the unknowing disciples for we already knew that he rose from the dead.

To show that this walk was like the one from the past, he read the appropriate selection from the Luke's Gospel: "That very same day, two of them were on their way to a village called Emmaus, seven miles from Jerusalem, and they were talking together about all that had happened. Now as they talked this over, Jesus himself came up and walked by their side; but something prevented them from recognizing him. He said to them, 'What matters are you discussing as you walk along?'

"They stopped short, their faces downcast. Then one of them, called Cleopas, answered him, 'You must be the only person staying in Jerusalem who does not know the things that have been happening there these last few days. . . Then he [Jesus] said to them, 'You foolish men! So slow to believe the full message of the prophets!'... Now while he was with them at table, he took the bread and said the blessing; then he broke it and handed it to them... Then they said to each other, 'Did not our hearts burn within us as he talked to us on the road and explained the scriptures to us'?"

"I like this story very much," Frater Jerome noted, "especially that there was something burning in their hearts when Jesus was present although they did not recognize him. I guess they were still in the throes of despair after his death on the cross. What I like is that they went from despair with their hearts burning to a new awareness and delight in the Lord's presence."

"This walk will be a mini-pilgrimage," Father Martin stated, "comparable only in a minor way to Emmaus and to Camino de Santiago in Spain." He built on the experience of those in the abbacy who went yearly on a pilgrimage to Our Lady of Mount Carmel. "To that pilgrimage, the prairie people went and still go with cars, although in early days some walked miles to this place. They go to confession, sing hymns, celebrate Holy Mass with fellow pilgrims; they pray for a successful harvest; it is an opportunity to gain indulgences.

"After the celebration of the Mass on Mount Carmel, there is a noon break as pilgrims make their way to their cars and their packed meals. After that, they process with the Blessed Sacrament and walk the stations of the cross at the base of the mount. There is a little hardship involved in this pilgrimage for it could occur on a hot summer day. This area of Carmel is a stony and sometimes arid land and if the pilgrimage occurs late in the month, we could see some stooks around the processional route.

"In medieval times pilgrims could exert great physical effort and encounter dangerous wild animals and bad weather. One could become ill, be subjected to violence, hunger and exhaustion. Those who go on the Camino today write about stepping on fecal matter, being subject to the sights of poverty and the smells of farms.

"But being on the way," Father Martin underlined, "can help us to learn to pray with renewed fervor. It can be a time of simplicity during which we can form bonds with the land, animals, birds, and become centered and focused on God. Step by step, our feet and faith can become connected."

"Was Father Martin being too romantic and poetic?" Frater Tobias pondered.

So here we were, the very next day after Easter Sunday and after the morning Masses; we were walking to the neighboring parish of St. Alban about four miles away. We had dressed well, with parkas and toques for there was frost in the air. Someone had forgotten to go to the bathroom before embarking. He darted into the woods for his necessary business, more than for a leak, because he called for paper. But we had only hard paper, the notes for our trip, not even more pliable dollar bills. "Use old leaves," someone shouted.

"It's okay to stay in the woods for a little while, but later on the wood tics can be really bad," Father Martin observed. "I don't think they are out yet."

Along the way, Frater Jerome's shoe laces came undone. He stopped, sat on the shoulder of the road and began tying them again. "Did you get a flat tire?" Frater Leo inquired jokingly. "If so, use your spare!"

I marveled at nature as we walked along; it was so much like our farm. Green grass and fields of stubble formed the bottom layer. Dead grass and shrubs were the next layer. Saplings and mature trees rose up and embraced the sky. Here was a community of nature.

"Welcome to our parish," Father Conrad, the German pastor greeted us. "I am sure it is good to get out of your musty novitiate. You must be tired after walking so far. Rest a little; we will eat some wiener schnitzel or bratwurst, take your pick, or eat both, some sauerkraut, and drink a stein of beer. Then I will tell you about our round song, Schnitzelbank. It is very lively and a good way to learn German. Even if your background is not German, you can easily sing it."

After the group finished eating and drinking like Germans, Father Conrad moved to the large chart containing the words of the song and started explaining it. He told us he had prepared for our visit. Maybe Father Conrad had too much beer, but he told us novices that he had showered in his underwear so as to not look down on his unemployed workers!

He got to the poster. "A *schnitzelbank* is a woodworking bench where you can sit and use a foot-operated vise. See this chart. It gives all the symbols and words. Most of the words are obvious from the illustrations, but just to describe some of the more difficult ones: an *Ochsenblas* is shown here as an ox bladder, but it actually means ox blast, or ox fart. A *Schnickelfritz* means a little rascal. *Tannenbaum* is a fir tree, not really a Christmas one.

"I will give you the English translation, but we must sing it in German to get its spirit and rhythm. So, after lots of German food and beer, we are ready to go. Give it your best."

Father Conrad pointed to each item on the chart: "I will sing it first."

1. Ist das nicht ein Schnitzelbank? Ja das ist ein Schnitzelbank.
Oh du schöne, oh du schöne Schnitzelbank.
2. Ist das nicht ein kurz und lang? Ja das ist ein kurz und lang.
3. Ist das nicht ein hin und her? Ja das ist ein hin und her.
Hin und her, kurz und lang,
Oh du schöne, oh du schöne Schnitzelbank.
4. Ist das nicht ein kreuz und quer? Ja das ist ein kreuz und quer.
5.Ist das nicht ein Schiessgewehr? Ja das ist ein Schiessgewehr.
Schiessgewehr, kreuz und quer, hin und her, kurz und lang,
Oh du schöne, oh du schöne Schnitzelbank.
6. . . . Judenmeier
. . . grose Eier
7. . . . grosses Glass
. . . Ochsenblas
8. . . . Haufen Mist
. . . Schnickelfritz
9. . . . dicke Frau
. . . fette Sau
10. . . . langer Mann
. . . Tannenbaum
11. . . . Hochzeitsring
. . . gefährliches Ding
1. Is that not a carving bench?
Yes that is a carving bench.
Oh you, oh you wonderful carving bench.
2. Is that not a short and long?
Yes that is a short and long.
3. Is that not a here and there?
Yes that is a here and there.
Here and there, short and long,
Oh you, oh you wonderful carving bench.
4. Is that not a crooked and straight?
Yes that is a crooked and straight.
5. Is that not a shooting gun?
Yes that is a shooting gun.
Shooting gun, crooked and straight, here and there, short and long.
Oh you, oh you wonderful carving bench.
6. . . . a Jew
. . . big egg
7. . . . big glass
. . . oxen fart
8. . . . pile of manure
. . . mischievous boy

9. . . . stout woman
. . . fat sow
10. . . . tall man
. . . fir tree
11. . . . wedding ring
. . . dangerous thing

"Thanks for singing so lustily! Now you're on your walk again. Jesus has accompanied you, shared with you his German food and beer and sang with us. Maybe one of you will conduct this Schnitzelbank in this parish in the future."

As the novices were walking back to the abbey, Frater Jerome said he was disturbed by the reference the Schnitzelbank song made to a Jew. He was not sure what the name, *Judenmeier* meant, but joining it with a big egg and the illustration of a Jewish male with a large nose, rustic sideburns and a skull cap did not sit well with him.

"Jesus was a Jew and I don't think we should show a Jew like this," he remarked. "If our Christian origins are in Judaism, we should have positive words about them, focus on a unity with them, not on what divides us but on something we have in common."

"The references were also to a lot of barnyard stuff," Frater Tobias remarked. "But that is all right for I did a lot of manuring of barns on our farm and I smelled many animal farts."

"I guess we are a little critical about this German song but I don't like to think of my mother as a big momma, certainly not as a fat sow, although she was not a slim woman," Frater Leo remarked.

On this walk two of us strayed off the road into a meadow. There was a bit of ice and snow in the lower regions, a few tiny rivulets, but the gopher mounds and hills were already bare from the spring sun. In that mostly cool terrain, I spotted a flash of violet, standing defiantly among withered grass blades. Their colored hues had broken through the prairie grasses still sleeping in the unbroken soil.

I welcomed their lavender petals, their outstretched arms guzzling up the rays of the sun. These crocuses were brave and bold friends, beguiling in their bloom. What independent characters, willing to demonstrate life and seasonal change! How can I describe these charming soft blue creatures with bronzy yellow stems and the fragrance of vanilla and cinnamon. They lift up my spirits.

"You are really in love with these flowers," Frater Leo remarked. "I like them too, but I think they smell like tobacco."

"That sounds gross," Frater Tobias retorted. "I bet we are talking about the same flowers that I heard about in the *Song of Songs*."

The novices were invigorated by the walk, food, singing and the flowers. During the evening Vesper service, they dozed a little but were ready for supper.

Teachings on the mystical body and liturgy

FATHER ABBOT LECTURED TO the novices once a week when he was able. We novices got the indication that the Abbot considered himself as the only real novice master, but because of his many duties and his age, he gave part of his task to the associate master of novices, and to the keeper of gardens who assigned outside duties.

The novices who had attended the college were told that all of the incoming and outgoing mail, for the college and for the monks, was scrutinized by the Abbot himself. One student who thought he would obviously be chosen to become a novice, had printed notices of the ceremony and date of his investiture as a novice. But the Abbot thought he would not make a good monk and so rejected him. No notices were sent.

As a sign of reverence when the Abbot entered the room for his talk, all of us novices stood, and sat down only after he did. In his first session, he distributed to each novice a black, hard-covered volume with a small gold sticker of the Sacred Heart on the front. In it he himself had bound together the two encyclical letters of Pope Pius XII, one, *Mystici Corporis* (The Mystical Body of Christ), 1943, and the second, *Mediator Dei,* (The Sacred Liturgy), 1947. The Abbot inserted a personally typed page into each volume–a commentary on the sacred liturgy by Rev. Gerald Ellard, SJ. He also penned in corrections to the English translations of the original Latin.

As the Abbot proudly presented each novice with a copy of the bound volume, he indicated that his talks would focus on the contents of these important encyclicals. The novices found out later that the Abbot's talks were really based on notes he received from his friend and liturgical pioneer in the United States, Rev. Virgil Michel.

Father Michel indicated that the liturgical apostolate was a continuation of the church through time. He outlined the spiritual nature of the church rather than merely her legal aspects. Celebration of the church's rituals was more than a submission to the rules and religious formulas. There should be a movement to go back to the Gospels, to early traditions and also to the spirit of the founders. Christians were to be active, rather than passive, not just pray and pay, for a mostly passive response indicates they are really not lay apostles.

"Since the celebration of the Mass is the true source of Christian spirit," Father Abbot stated, "the lay people are to be active here also, answering the prayers and singing where appropriate. For if Catholics are merely passive in the liturgy, they most likely will be passive outside the liturgy as well. Being a Catholic means more than merely avoiding mortal sin. Baptism is more than merely ending the state of separation from God by washing away original sin; it is more than the forgiveness of sin for it means the engrafting of a human being into the living vine that is Christ.

"Through baptism and the sacraments, Christ Jesus is a brother," the Abbot emphasized, focusing on the encyclical's original word for brothers, *consanguineis,* joined/mixed with the blood of Christ. Relying on the encyclical on the mystical body, he defined the true church as one, holy, Catholic, apostolic, and Roman. The Holy Spirit lives and works in all its members.

Baptism is not merely a past event but a seed, a beginning that must grow. In this celebration and in everyday work, there is a sharing in the priesthood of Christ. "In the Church, individual members do not live for themselves alone, but also help their fellows toward the more perfect building up of the whole body," the encyclical stated.

Liturgy is the exercise and continuation of the priesthood of Christ, in his mystical body through the Mass, sacraments, and the Divine Office. Liturgy is the life of the church.

The Abbot was clear in demonstrating that while baptism is common to both priests and laymen, they have different roles in the liturgy. It is the priest alone who can change the bread and wine into the body and blood of Christ. The priest both confects and offers the sacrifice, a process that theologians call *transubtantiation.* The lay people do not confect, but join with the priest in making the offering. They are not co-celebrants but co-offerers. This was of eminent importance for the Abbot, since it is here that he typed and inserted a specific commentary by Father Ellis.

Especially pertinent to Benedictines was the Pope's section on the Divine Office, the perennial prayer of the church. This Office is "the prayer of the Mystical Body of Jesus Christ, offered to God in the name and on behalf of all Christians, when recited by priests and other ministers of the Church and by religious who are deputed by the Church for this."

We listened attentively but were surrounded in mystery. "Wow, a lot for us to assimilate!" Frater Callistus concluded during recreation time.

The Abbot sat quite authoritatively in his chair, generally closed his eyes, often became rapturously involved in what he was saying and gesticulated to the ceiling. He did not invite any questions and when Frater Tobias once asked for a clarification of what he said, the Abbot misconstrued it to involve a questioning of doctrine. Consequently, he became quite distraught and indicated that this seeming questioning of doctrine indicated a lack of faith and could lead to dismissal.

"When he stared at me and became so disturbed at my question, I thought he was going to send me to hell," Frater Tobias reflected.

"In some of my university classes we were invited to give responses to the prescribed text, to questions the teacher posed," Frater Jerome observed. "But it is evident that we are to be passive in the Abbot's class. I was alarmed when he suggested that Frater Tobias could be kicked out for apparently asking an innocent question, a clarification really."

"If the true church is only Roman and those are the only ones going to be saved, I wonder about some of my relatives who are Protestant and some who don't believe at all," Frater Jerome remarked. "I really don't want to be separated from them in the afterlife. But I still think the Abbot is a great guy!"

There was, however, one annoying habit that Father Abbot had when he gave his talks. As he sat behind his lecturing table, and when he was not gesticulating to the heavens, he scratched on an opening on the table top. This grating sound distracted us from his message for it continued from class to class. Finally, we decided to do something about it—we turned the table around so that the crack was no longer available. Father Abbot came in next class, sat down and repeatedly searched for the fissure but found none. The noise problem was solved!

More on the liturgy

FATHER MARTIN FOLLOWED UP on the Abbot's remarks on the liturgy. At least ideally, he stated, Benedictine monks mark time not by hours, days, or decades, but by the liturgical year, the church's seasons of the year. Monks do not regulate their lives so much by their watches or the calendar, not by business opportunities or social engagements, but by the wake-up bell to come to monastic prayers, and, later in the day, by the tolling of the angelus bell.

The prayers of the monastic Office give a structure to the days and nights. Time should move unhurriedly. For a monk, in some ways there is no future, and no past but merely a series of nows, one moment followed by another like a heartbeat. For the monk, time should slow down with monks living leisurely. There is no need to keep up with the Joneses, no need to worry about what one should wear or what one should make for dinner. Instead, with all this relatively unstructured time, monks can pray and reflect; they have time and silence to live deeper.

"There are layers of concentric circles that wrap novices and professed monks and, at least ideally, envelope them in prayer and closeness to God," Father Martin stated. "The outermost circle is the monastic land and farm; the walls of the monastery are the second circle, and the inner and third circle are the chapel and monastic cells. This last circle is very precious and, as you can see especially for you novices, there are few worldly distractions: no magazines, television, newspapers (except the *Prairie Messenger!*), no secular books, telephones, radios, or even musical instruments. This enclosed circle provides a time to reflect, to consider what is important, to grow as a monk and as a human being. As you can see, our values are not part of everyday culture; our way of life forms a bulwark against humanity's digressions; in many ways we are witnesses to a counter culture."

Hermit life

"THE COENOBITIC OR COMMUNITY model of the Benedictines and their successors is derived from eremitism, that is, living a solitary life," Father Martin said in one of his lectures. "While living alone is great, and can lead to holiness, it is not the way we live, for we are foremost a community."

As we novices cut down trees on the south side of the monastery grounds, we perceived some small houses. They were the dwelling places of hermits, those living a solitary life. One of these dwellings had a tabernacle and bread from the altar, and hermits came to worship there, but these solitaries generally came to the monastic Mass each morning.

A former Carthusian monk and three former religious Sisters inhabited these separate buildings. One of the Benedictines also decided to lead a solitary life. Father Vincent had been very actively involved in monastic activities; he was editor of the monastic-based paper for 10 years and teacher both in high school and college for 20 years. He was a very congenial person, often joking with guests and fellow monks.

But he rather suddenly decided to go solitary. He approached the Abbot who had a penchant for the solitary life himself, having as his motto, *Soli Deo,* for God alone. The Abbot thought this new vocation over with Father Vincent and concluded that his motives were pure and honorable. If Father Vincent wanted to pursue the eremitical life, that of a hermit, he would have to find another suitable building. There was a granary on the farm premises but it was not bourgeois enough, that is, it was not sufficiently insulated, had a poor provision for heating and only single-pane windows.

Father Abbot approached the business manager of the abbey to help provide a proper eremitical house and he learned of a vacated one in the nearby town. He purchased that dwelling and had it moved onto the abbey premises, in an area quite accessible to the monastery but removed from main traffic and at a sufficient distance from other dwellings. A location near the orchard seemed perfect. A natural gas line was routed there and an electrical line strung. The main hardship seemed to be the lack of an indoor toilet so an outside biffy had to do!

Father Vincent checked every day on the progress of adding double-pane windows to the building and insulating and wiring it. Brother Wolfgang, an adept carpenter, was in charge. Progress proceeded apace and Father Vincent relocated there without fanfare.

Although Father Vincent had the approval of his superior for such a venture, he could not find any specific rules for solitaries akin to those for monastic and religious communities such as the *Rule of St. Benedict*.

"I guess I have to find out what authentic solitary life should be like, otherwise I will have to make it up myself," he noted. As he progressed in his new vocation, he began to appropriate many of the eremitical ideals, at least in theory.

"The greatest obstacle to this way of life is myself," he confessed. "I have to come to grips with my failures and my aspirations."

As he progressed in his reflections, generally beyond the molting stages, he agreed to share them with his monastic community which included the novices. During these talks, he traced his initial rationale for joining the monastic community.

"My present venture into solitude follows closely, I think, my monastic vocation. I still remain a monk, but now with a new bent. I remain convinced that our age and Protestantism in general needs the monastery. It helps us as Christians to focus on what is essential for Christianity. I like the analogy from the Danish philosopher, Soren Kierkegaard, a Lutheran: Monasticism is like a buoy for those navigating at sea; this buoy makes it possible to locate where we are. I think I have found that buoy and now see it also in the hermit life.

"Being a hermit is not for everyone, not for every monk. It is a radical step and I hope for the grace to pursue it and remain with it for a while. For me, I have taken the vow of poverty, but this hermit life is an even more radical step. Although fellow monks have teased me that I will become bourgeois since I will have electricity and natural gas, I will have to face myself and what it means to be a solitary focused on the Gospels and the Rule.

"I have concluded that this radical life means doing nothing, at least not defining myself in terms of what I do, so that when someone asks me what I am doing, I will reply, Nothing. Well, I will still be doing something: reviewing books, teaching a class, weeding in the garden, getting food from the kitchen unlike the solitaries of old who were self-sufficient, taking a shower. But my vocation will be more radical than that: I will try to do nothing. I will focus on the radical other. I realize that mine is a rare vocation, only for a few. It is a privilege and quite far removed from the hermits of old.

"I have lived in a solitary cell, a room, in the monastery for quite a long time. But my jobs as teacher and editor and my monastic life have involved me with the outside world and with fellow monks. I have seldom been alone for a long period of time. Now I have to cultivate being alone and I am a little apprehensive about it even though I have chosen it.

"I have begun by learning to live in the dark. In the evening, after I have finished my breviary, I turn out the lights and soak in the darkness and become enveloped in it. Such a conscious feeling is new for me. I try and manage and fumble around in the dark as I get ready for bed. This experience is coupled with the fading light in the fall and winter as the days get shorter and push inside me. I associate this feeling with crumpled leaves, drying and dead, with the cold and biting wind. Can I be changed by being alone and in the dark?

"There is a tradition that monastic life is merely the beginning of a Christian life and that being a solitary is the pinnacle of being a Christian. I accept this in theory for I would be a fool to think I am leading a more perfect life. I should be the last to have such an aspiration.

"I prayed Psalm 92 which inveighs against the wicked and also against the senseless fool and is in favor of the righteous who will produce fruit in old age and praise Yahweh who is the upright rock. I am that fool and hope to praise Yahweh nevertheless."

Night lights

WHILE IN THE MONASTIC choir, a verse of *Psalm 119* struck me especially: "As your words unfold, it gives light and the simple understand." There were few bright electrical lights in the monastery, and in the evening all of them were turned off for the diesel engine generating electricity stopped functioning. Small night lights provided a path in the darkness.

At first, I didn't understand the implications of the psalmist that the Lord's light unfolds, but the image of light hit me and reminded me of the lights on our farm. In the early days we did not have electricity in our house and barn, just as my grandparents were bereft if it on their homesteads. But when my parents went to Toronto to work, they were immersed in electrical light. So, when they returned to the farm, they knew that electrical currents were possible.

Before their brief exodus to central Canada, my parents had to rely on coal oil or kerosene lamps and lanterns, both in the house and when walking to the barn, while feeding the horses and cattle, and while milking the cows. We called the lights used outside the house, lanterns, and those inside, lamps. Portable hand-held lanterns often burned with a smoky flame, especially when there was air movement. Mom then had to trim the flat cotton wick and clean the glass chimney or globe.

So, I made connections between the lighting in the monastery and that experienced at home. Both of them dispelled the physical darkness, but the Lord's words were a light uncovering for me, the simple one, levels of understanding of the many facets of monastic life.

Less than serious talk

ALL FOUR OF US were given the afternoon detail once again of hoeing the weeds around the fruit trees in the orchard. The crabapples were too green to eat so we engaged in some rather trivial talk. We did not follow the *Tyrocinium's* suggestion that we converse on spiritual matters alone. Instead, most of us engaged in worldly and even incidental topics, this time about motor vehicles. We radiated the values of our families on their purchases and reliance on specific cars.

Frater Tobias waxed eloquent about the best of cars, a 1950 Ford Meteor. As you know, it was Henry Ford who put North America on its wheels. He made it possible for the average wage-earner and farmer to own a vehicle, first the Model T and then the Model A. He established a motor plant in Windsor, Ontario, and had markets throughout the British Empire. These first cars were really sturdy and could handle rough roads.

"Let me tell you about our recent and first family car. Our Meteor is blue in color and has a sun visor. Really has lots of room in it and vinyl seat covers. 'Be miles ahead with Meteor,' I remember an ad saying. 'Lean back and relax at the wheel of a Meteor. Deft, obedient steering. Swift, sure, gentle braking. Low-to-the road stability. Relax in deep, roomy, five-foot seats. Picture-window visibility. Wide doors, great spacious luggage compartments. Soft, smooth ride. Built-in ventilating system. Low, wide, youthful lines. Thirteen thrilling body colors and combinations.' You get the picture."

For Frater Leo it was pride in Chrysler's DeSoto. Reliable and flamboyant.

For Frater Jerome it was an esthetically pleasing Chevrolet.

For Frater Callistus there were two important vehicles: the Volkswagen beetle and the bullet nose Studebaker. "The bug or beetle kept its original design, a worthy being, but over the years it made many rather incidental changes; it combined its being with becoming. See, I learned something from philosophy classes! But I also like the prominent schnoz of the Studebaker and its grille, opening into a smile. It is definitely ahead of its time and its body style nothing short of sensational."

BATHROOM EXPERIENCES

As I woke up, I was still groggy and went to the water closet on the main floor. It was used by all the monks including the novices. I was standing in this full-length floor standing urinal doing my job. There was no privacy wall and I was next to a yawning confrere.

The urinal had no flushing device and so I was startled when I felt some liquid streaming down my leg into my slipper. No, it was not from the urinal for it was warm and emanated from a human device belonging to my confrere. I groaned, motioned to him and he pushed his spigot in the proper direction, hardly noticing the impropriety. I quickly finished my job and went to the basins and grabbed a paper towel to dry my shank and slipper. Needless to say, I was now more awake than before and noticed my confrere slink out of the bathroom.

A novice confrere confided to me that he developed the habit of crapping only once a week. "It certainly saves a lot of time although I get a rather full feeling near the end of seven days," he noted. "Some have noticed that I have a rather large belly and rear end. Maybe I am eating too many chocolate bars. This is the seventh day and I will inhabit the toilet stall for some time for this bowel movement. It is quite a bit to unload and the stench becomes great. I have to do a lot of straining and I am told that I might do some intestinal damage. I hope the toilet can take the poop although I do flush it periodically in the process.

"I was told that my condition is that of constipation and that I lack fiber in my diet for fiber stores up water in my stool. I was told that my condition can lead to hemorrhoids and some serious diseases. It is true that sometimes I have to take laxatives. Still, I am not about to change my unusual habit."

BEDS

Novices heard that some monks slept on boards, that is, on a mattress supported by boards. One cited health reasons for this practice, for a firm foundation for one's back aided its proper functioning. Another chose these boards for ascetic reasons, that is, to make a sacrifice rather than pamper oneself. This practice also was in tune with St. Benedict's day and earlier. Frater Leo was never convinced of these ascetic ways. "I used to like the most cushy bed and generally slept in the nude; that was a more natural way of doing things, even in the winter."

STORE ROOM

There was a supply/store room for the monks which had some new under-clothes but also contained those gathered from deceased monks. Initially the novices wore the undershirts, trousers, socks and shoes that they had when they came to the monastery.

One of the monks, Father William became irked by some of the apparel that the young initiates had. He should have voiced his complaints to the Abbot, the Socius or the novice master, but instead he stopped individuals and complained that their shoes made too much noise or that their socks were white. "Are you trying to show off?" he complained. While some novices were wearing socks they had before coming to the monastery, others had actually procured these from the store room.

The future

IN A CHANCE MEETING with one of the monks studying for the priesthood, the four of us started talking about life after the year's novitiate. He was a very practical minded sort. He did not tell us about the program of philosophical studies, but encouraged us to learn how to type. It was a sine-qua-non skill, he judged, since the term paper required for each class had to be in a typed format. He encouraged us to learn touch typing proficiently by disciplining ourselves to follow a method given in a book for beginners, requiring only ten minutes each and every day. We obeyed. Quite a noise in the novitiate!

The manual promised that in no time I could type the sentence, Now is the time for all good men to come to the aid of the party. I had tried the hunt and peck approach before; I looked at the keyboard and used only my index fingers. But now I was convinced of the worth of this new method. I slaved through the boring repetitive exercise, jik, jik, jik over and over again. I learned to type faster.

This touch typing or blind typing had to be learned. I had to use all of my fingers, including my thumbs. I became quite accurate, increased my speed and reduced my mental fatigue for I no longer looked at my fingers. Instead, I concentrated on what I was doing, the text. I worked on the letters first and later learned the numbers, punctuation marks and symbols, margin setting, paragraph indentation and how to replace a ribbon.

Now each of my fingers had its own keyboard zone. My hands did not dance across the keyboard but were fixed in one position. Only my fingers moved, stretching in different directions; they came to know in which direction to go.

The Remington typewriter I used made both my body and my brain work hard. The muscles in my fingers particularly in my pinky grew in strength. I drew out the content; I pounded out sentences; it was satisfying: the flipping of fingers, the dinging bell, the snap, snap, snap of the keys.

Frater Jerome made his typing sing. It was his touch, gentle and rhythmic.

Frater Leo made the machine sprout wings and it would really fly often in anger. For Frater Callistus the writing machine was deliberate as if searching for the right word or phrase.

But for me the finished product was cold and impersonal; it was mechanical writing and so I wrote by hand to my parents and siblings. There were benefits to the old-fashioned way of writing with pen or pencil and paper. I sharpened my brain as I recalled and remembered my experiences. There was a link between my arm movement and its ability to enhance creativity. As I formed words, I remembered to put into practice the handwriting skills I learned in grade school; it was called improving penmanship. In handwriting I had to focus on the actual writing process; it was slow and allowed me time to process my thoughts, develop my ideas as I visualized them in written form. In fact, handwriting was a meditative and peaceful way of communicating. For me, the pen was still mightier than the sword!

The novitiate provided many challenges. Father Martin spoke about the cloud of unknowing. We tried to understand it, for it pertained to our present life. We often felt hemmed in; we were not free to move about, to pursue ways of life we knew before.

We knew we had to pray and work, the Benedictine motto–*ora et labora*–and that whatever holy things or ordinary things we were doing were for the glory of God, again, another Benedictine saying, *ut in omnibus glorificetur Deus*, that in all things God might be glorified. After all, Jacob wrestled with the angel from five different perspectives. And we were doing this in a cloister of monks.

But where was this leading us? It was a spiritual process, we were told; we were to trust that somehow this was a better life than most Christians lived. We were living a Christian life which already had great merit, but we were also looking forward to taking vows which would add even greater merit. Then we would be living out not only our Christian lives but also living according to the vows, the vows of religion.

Frater Callistus joked about his feeling that the monastery hemmed him in. "Ever hear the one about the monk and the prisoner? The prison guard asked both the same question: How long are you in for? The prisoner answered, for life, for killing someone. The monk answered, I also am in for life, for taking vows! Maybe this life of isolation is not the best thing? It could be psychologically damaging.

"I am trying to find myself, to find what I should do, to find where I should be. Maybe I can take some cues from the Bible. Moses had many rebuffs but the burning bush showed him how serious God was about his leading the people. Samuel's calling came from a dream, someone calling him in rather inaudible whispers, and his response, 'Here I am Lord. Tell me what to do.'

"Paul was thrown to his knees on his way to Damascus and told to radically alter his ways. I don't expect such dramatic flares, but how can I really know? The way in the monastery is kind of set; it is ordination to the priesthood, but I have to grapple with what is inside me now."

There were other challenges besides a feeling of being imprisoned. Some felt getting up so early in the morning really challenging. Sleeping in an extra 20 minutes on Sunday did not cut it. Some could not bear the cold and the noise of radiators clanging every morning. Others languished from loneliness and felt that their life was wasting away for they were not preparing for something specific in life, a skill.

But all of these intangibles were part of the nature of being a novice, being a monk. It was a spiritual process. Some began to question the nature of vocation in general and that of a monk in particular. All vocations had difficulty, some more than others. It became clear that there was something special about this vocation and whether it fits a specific individual or not.

Obviously not everyone was destined to become a monk, but some were. How does one know that? For those whom it fit, they had to find that out. If it fit, then they might desire it. One novice liked the Benedictine habit more than the floppy and brown Franciscan one. But clothing alone cannot or should not determine a vocation. It has to be a personal calling which goes beyond some fascination and desire. It has to be about something important, more important than the way clothes look. What was involved in a monk's vocation? St. Benedict emphasized prayer. That was very important, the center. Having a prayerful disposition and praying a lot made sense.

"Praying will help me grow as an individual and in my relation to fellow monks," Frater Tobias reflected. "What I do besides praying may not be that important. So what I do in the monastery becomes secondary to the primary vocation. If I engage in praying, I will not be wasting my time; I will not be missing out on things that others do; they live well on the outside with another vocation. I have to learn to be myself, not someone else."

CLOSING THE MONASTERY?

It seemed strange to Frater Callistus that the novice master pinned a duty on these novices, one which ran counter to Frater Callistus' conniving motives. The duty these novices had was to ensure the continuance of the monastery by praying daily for more vocations in general, but specifically, that the novitiate be filled with monks in the coming year. It was a little hard to do this through direct contacts, but the novices could pray for such vocations.

The specific saint Father Martin suggested to petition was Sister Fortunata Viti, a nineteenth-century Benedictine. He provided a prayer card which had her image on it. She was a Benedictine for seventy years, remained illiterate, and served her community as a housekeeper, spinning, sewing, washing and mending. She had a great devotion to the Blessed Sacrament. One story was that she began to cry during a Mass because she felt that the celebrating priest would leave the priesthood and she had sorrow for him. After her death, miracles were reported at her graveside.

Frater Callistus was a calculating novice. He had been like that before he entered the monastery. In grade school, he liked mathematics, liked surpassing his fellow students in adding and subtracting. In college, he took calculus and accounting classes, ending with a Bachelor of Commerce degree. This reasoning and planning process continued as part of his character as he began the novitiate and he was quite vocal about it with his fellow novices, not with his superiors, however.

"I know that my motivation is perhaps not the noblest," he confessed to Frater Leo. "In college, I did not bother too much with religion and I noticed that even the most fervent in the beginning started to slack off in practice. I think this cooling off of fervor is present in society in general and it will take place in the monastery also. While four novices in the novitiate is quite a few and will keep the place going for some time, especially if all of us stay, the greater number in this monastery are quite old and getting older; this place is in some way a museum piece or an old folks' home.

"My intentions are not the purest, but I can envision that after a while there will be very few monks to run the place and those few will have to take care of the weak and sick. I know that the farm has a productive dairy herd at present, a noisy piggery and lots of eggs from the chickens. But in time all of these enterprises will close as the monks get more crotchety and unable to take care of them.

"Maybe there will be time when most of the monks will be so old that the authorities will forbid them to admit new applicants because there will no longer be anyone to engage in their formation. That is where I and maybe one or two others will come in. We will have the opportunity to take over the monastery, sell it if we wish, and live happily ever after.

"Maybe this thinking is a little crass and mercenary. But I notice that even now the middle-aged and older monks are showing their age. Some limp a bit; a few use canes to steady their walk. Some cannot see or hear too well for being old comes with baggage.

"The elderly rule the monastery. I know that some of these monks have done a lot for me during my year in college, but they are fossil heads, relics. These are harsh words but these older monks should leave a lot more in the hands of the young who have more creativity, imagination and ener-gy. According to the Rule and the Bible, the mere boys, Samuel and Daniel, judged the priests.

"The older have important experiences but have a preservation men-tality and are set in their ways. They often have a regressive view of things, like the type of prayer used, the early time for waking, and very traditional types of food. They have been around forever, have cast the rules, and have been elected by older members and continue to re-elect them. Look at the Abbot; he has a stranglehold on power and continuance; he sees that his job is like that of a biological parent who can never disown and leave his children. It is an anachronistic view for no one should stay in an elected position for life; it merely keeps gerontocracy alive.

"Give the young a chance, a chance even to make their own mistakes, otherwise the monastery will die, like a family with no children. It will be the end of the line, no more applicants, death. I heard that some monks wanted to develop their talents and were given encouragement from the outside. I was told of a biologist who was doing original research into water insects up North. He was enthusiastic about the importance of his findings, but superi-ors discouraged him, stifled him, and gave him pastoral tasks instead.

"So I am in a bind: on the one hand, in joining this community, I am helping to ensure its continuance; on the other, I am selfishly hoping for its discontinuance so that I can take it over and manage it. This death will be a good thing, just as Jesus died on Calvary and then rose. Where there is death there is hope.

"I don't see myself as one of the regular types in this novitiate or in the monastery. I might not be very stable and quite insecure, but my ideas might lead to some interesting achievements."

Frater Callistus became more explicit in his negativity, this time very personal. After a few months in the novitiate, he vented his frustration. "I thought the monastery was a place where we could pursue intellectual and cultural things. I had so many monastic aspirations and was told to never set limits, go after your dreams, don't be afraid to push the boundaries. There will be suffering and pain in Christian life but also joy; sometimes you will be enmeshed in a circle of thorns. Toil and effort should result in a positive result.

"While I am complaining I will continue: although I experience a strange peace while meditating, there are constant interruptions; I do not get a quiet disposition because my confrere is snoring again. The food is luke-warm and boring. When I express my thoughts, and spiritual musings, I am misunderstood. When I do something well, I don't get sufficient credit for it.

"Instead, of doing exciting and cultural things, we mostly do boring stuff and physical work. I am very disappointed and on reflection am tend-ing to do things at most in a half-hearted sort of way. I am really not excited about anything any more. I still do the prayers and some reading but I am not enthusiastic about them.

"I thought we would spend a lot of time trying to understand the psalms since we pray them many times a day. But, no, instead of savoring their treasures, we have to copy in long hand a dry commentary on them."

To indicate that he was indeed different and indifferent, and in this instance frustrated, Frater Callistus started growing a beard. When the beard became noticeable, the novice master did not seem to mind and as it eventually grew it even demonstrated a way it might develop. There were, after all members of the community with beards and pictures of past bearded monks.

Maybe some of us are already losing it, for yesterday Frater Jerome told us he had lost his glasses. He was certain he had used them a few minutes be-fore. All of us dropped our tasks and searched for those spectacles. We looked in the obvious places but could not find them. Exhausted and frustrated, we sat down only to notice that all of this time they were on top of Frater Jerome's head! We thought all of us were going crazy and laughed a lot.

Conclusion

THERE WERE MANY EXTRAORDINARY things in this first year of monastic life. I liked the fellowship with my three novices and the embrace of the community during prayers and community repasts. We had a great sense of camaraderie whether it was during our daily walks, our work schedules and even our jostling during card games. I had not expected some of the experiences such as the daily meditation and our reading of the Latin commentaries by the Fathers of the Church during prayers. I was surprised by the frankness of my confreres particularly about their sexual exploits.

I learned a lot about myself too. It was a formative year and left a permanent stamp on me. Generally, the stamp was a positive one. I had to keep things in perspective and certainly that made me a more compassionate person.

I had to accept myself as I was, both as one who liked order but also one who needed some chaos to move into uncharted areas. I had to get used to institutional food, the expectation of the community for promptness and thoroughness.

I also had to be tolerant of others, that they were wonderful but also capable of godawful things–from getting used to others' stinky feet, to their constantly finding flaws in what I did, like not singing the Martyrology perfectly with a quint, to their objections of my mispronunciations of Latin, to listening to their sometimes boring stories. There were gruff answers and dry icing of my carefully crafted observations, some ill-will, all kinds of human stumbling blocks. Nothing in this place is very clean, dust is in the air, and the damp is pervasive and permanent, getting deeper into the walls each decade. Always there is the smell of sweaty, woolen habits. And a very pedestrian way of living,

Strangely, however, I was seduced by this life, but also acutely felt its physical discomforts. At home we had running water, but here each one of us had a basin on a stand with a crock pitcher. The water was always cold and had some ice in it during the winter months.

While I eventually got somewhat used to the early morning rising, I did not get the winter sleeping time I got on the farm. I think I grew with the men as the initial romance wore off, and the differences among us became apparent. In the end, I was enchanted by the monks who persevered in this life, but I also embraced those who left, who were monastic dropouts, fully sharing their relief.

As the official year of the novitiate wore on, a few novices had problems that began to surface. They asked questions such as: Am I cut out to lead a celibate life? Can I rise so early all the time for night/morning prayers that interrupt every night's sleep (granted there is an extra 20 minutes on Sunday morning!)? Can I continue to maintain such spiritual stamina all my life?

There was some glue to bind us together, however, a moral and spiritual solidarity we felt for each other and the troupe, and leaving meant leaving that groupiness.

"I am not sure I want to stay much longer than the novitiate," Frater Callistus reflected. "My expectations for the community are too materialistic. Maybe I'll bow out for it might be better for me to walk out instead of being carried out."

"My sexual leanings might not be acceptable to the community," Frater Leo judged. "Maybe I have been sleeping like Rip Van Winkle and when the truth be known, they might shun me. My talents might belong elsewhere. At the beginning, I felt that this was another world I was entering but I also thought it was the Lord who was leading me in and now he seems to be leading me out."

"Despite some misgivings and fear about the laws and order in this Benedictine community, it seems to be my cup of tea," Frater Tobias confessed. "I like the blend of direction and chaos even though there is a lot of austerity mixed in. It is a fulfilling but also an unfinished journey. But I have to be realistic. I go back to some negativities, some hard to take, others quite petulant. Ours is a regimen of eating in silence but some confreres did not pass me the food at table, despite my obvious sign requests.

"I have to endure disrespectful patronizing remarks about my innocent rural habits by more sophisticated city dwellers. We bickered and gossiped a lot, vaunted our superiority, stated our views too strongly, were reluctant to admit we were wrong, showed some ambition and competed with one another, despised laggards, practiced unmonkly attitudes and actions. I let my glances go astray, contrary to Father Martin's injunction to keep custody of the eyes.

"But I also tried to be understanding and compassionate, for some older monks made a lot of noise during the great silence; one snored during the homilies. A few avoided us, not even giving us a greeting. Some older monks appeared excessively pious, peaceful and still crotchety; their silence and piety brought them closer to God's love but, alas, it seemed that a good number of them became addled and severely antisocial.

"So, I delighted more in those who were not pious and jovial. I had to bring together both mine and their strengths and weaknesses, that those with moral failings could still have redemptive qualities and become whole. It is like swallowing a hot potato; I might like the potato but dislike its burning sensation. I gradually realized that human folly and weakness often nestle cheek by jowl with the divine."

Finally, a novice cracked and quickly rejoined his family. Another left because he discovered his homosexuality. Two of us remained to make temporary vows.

www.ingramcontent.com/pod-product-compliance
Lightning Source LLC
Chambersburg PA
CBHW060344100426
42812CB00003B/1122